D1477261

A Photo History of
ARMOURED
CARS
in Two World Wars

A Photo History of
ARMOURED CARS
in Two World Wars

George Forty

BLANDFORD PRESS

POOLE · DORSET

First published in the UK 1984 by Blandford Press,
Link House, West Street, Poole, Dorset BH15 1LL

Copyright © 1984 George Forty

Distributed in the United States by
Sterling Publishing Co., Inc.,
2 Park Avenue, New York, NY 10016

British Library Cataloguing in Publication Data

Forty, George
  A photo history of armoured cars in two
  world wars.
  1. Armored vehicles, Military—History
  I. Title
  623.74'75   UG446.5

  ISBN 0-7137-1215-5

Typeset by Keyspools Ltd, Golborne, Lancashire
Printed in Great Britain by BAS Printers Ltd.,
Wallop, Hampshire

Half-title page: **Daimler scout car.** Serving
with success in all theatres of war throughout
World War 2, 6,626 of this sturdy vehicle were
produced in three main marks, Marks I, Ia and
Ib, Mark II and Mark III. A Mark Ib is
illustrated in the Western Desert in 1942, along
with an M3 Stuart light tank.
Frontispiece: **Morris ad hoc armoured car,
1927.** This unique vehicle, locally built on a
Morris 6 × 4 truck chassis, was used by the
Singapore Volunteer Force in 1927.

Contents

Introduction

A Photohistory of Armoured Cars in Two World Wars is a companion volume to *A Photohistory of Tanks in Two World Wars*. Like that book, it is neither a dictionary nor an encyclopaedia, but is rather a pictorial evocation of armoured car design over its first 45 years. Unlike the subject of tanks, I do not believe that anyone has ever published such a wide-ranging collection of photographs of armoured cars which trace their development over nearly half a century. This book covers the fascinating early period before the start of World War 1; when the military potential of the horseless carriage was first appreciated. Armoured cars are far cheaper, easier to run and more versatile than tanks, especially for internal security and policing duties, and their somewhat restricted use during World War 1 was followed by a period of considerable activity. This was also a period of experimentation in design, and many interesting models were produced, including some from countries which were new in the armoured car field. Finally, the book covers the period of World War 2, when, once again, they were in and out of favour, largely depending upon the terrain in the area where they were used, but nowhere did they achieve the battlefield dominance of the tank.

Although the armoured car, being an armoured fighting vehicle, has the same basic characteristics as the tank, namely firepower, protection and mobility, the emphasis put upon each is very different. For example, firepower is the *raison d'être* for the tank, but for the armoured car it is instead just a means of getting it out of trouble. Fighting for information is a last resort. Although in some situations a lack of tank support has forced armoured cars to be used in their place, this is the exception rather than the rule. Crew protection can never be as good as that in a tank, because the generally lighter chassis of the armoured car just cannot carry the necessary weight of thick armour. Mobility on the other hand is of prime importance, so that the vehicle can travel quickly on roads and tracks and have a good range and endurance. Tracks, although inherently noisy, are more efficient than wheels on really bad going, but silence and stealth are most important factors in reconnaissance work and so wheels are favoured. In addition to these shifts of emphasis, another major characteristic must be added and that is flexibility. The mobility of the vehicles, their speed and endurance, the inherent ability of their crews and the enormous increase in efficiency and speed of reaction which radio communications bring, all make flexibility a major characteristic of armoured cars, made evident by the many and varied tasks which they are able to perform.

When compiling this book, the most difficult decision has not been what material to include but rather what to leave out. Does one, for example, cover armed motorcycles, gun carrying lorries or wheel-cum-track vehicles? What about scout cars, wheeled armoured personnel carriers and self propelled guns or half-tracks? All have some, but not all, of the characteristics of the armoured car, so merit inclusion. I have deliberately tried to put in as many different types of wheeled armoured fighting vehicles as possible, but at the same time clearly had to draw the line somewhere, or the book would have been enormous! Where necessary I have erred on the side of including something rather than leaving it out, which I hope will add spice to the mixture.

The majority of the photographs, with just a few exceptions, come from the remarkable collection owned by John Batchelor, the well-known graphic artist. They form but a small fraction of his immense collection and I am extremely indebted to him for their use. I must also thank the Tank Museum library for allowing me free access to their many books and pamphlets, and in particular to David Fletcher, the assistant librarian, for all his help and advice.

George Forty

Bryantspuddle,
November 1983

The Beginnings

'And the Lord was with Judah; and he drove out the inhabitants of the mountain, but he could not drive out the inhabitants of the valley, because they had chariots of iron.' These oft quoted words from the Book of Judges are describing the earliest direct ancestors of the armoured car, namely wheeled, animal-drawn war chariots, which date back to before 3000 BC. Clearly, the armoured car has an even stronger link with these early war machines than does the tank. However, like the tank, the first true armoured cars did not appear until this century, after the invention of the internal combustion engine had revolutionised road transport and made it possible to carry men, weapons and protective armour about on the battlefield at a reasonable speed. Armoured cars predate tanks by about ten to fifteen years, the first models appearing about the turn of the century, so they were established on the scene before the start of the Great War, albeit still very much in their infancy. As the photographs in this part of the book show, development on both sides of the Atlantic began using powered tricycles and quadricycles, but rapidly progressed onto more substantial chassis.

Early armoured cars were built or improvised to perform a variety of roles, with armed reconnaissance being quite low on the list, perhaps because this was still considered to be the task of others. Early German armoured cars, for example, were built as anti-balloon cannon-carrying vehicles, whose only role was to deal with the new menace from the air. Others had as their prime task the carrying of raiding parties, while some were there to rescue the pilots of aircraft which had crashed behind enemy lines. Many of these early cars were just civilian motor cars or lorries, with armour plate bolted on in strategic places, together with some form of vehicle-mounted weapon which could vary from a small pedestal-mounted machine gun to a large anti-aircraft gun.

Apart from the USA, which, despite some early enthusiasm, was never very keen on armoured cars, it was the larger, industrialised countries of Europe which were, not unnaturally, the only ones capable of producing these sophisticated machines. The first group were Austria, France, Germany, Great Britain and Italy. They were shortly joined by Belgium and Russia, although the latter made more use of other nations' armoured cars rather than producing anything very much for themselves.

Of these early vehicles, perhaps the 1904/05 Daimler Panzerwagen, built by Austria, is a good example to choose to illustrate the basic ingredients that make up the true armoured car. It had good mobility, which was enhanced over its civilian counterparts by having four-wheel drive, thus enabling it to motor with some success across relatively poor going, so that it was not confined to metalled roads. It had an armour plated hull to protect the crew, although the armour was not very thick. Finally, it had a fully traversing turret in which was mounted the main vehicle armament – in this case one or two Maxim machine guns, so it had respectable firepower, but not an excessive amount. It thus had mobility, protection and firepower, the essential basic ingredients and in the correct order of priority.

Armoured cars first saw action in 1912, when the Italians used some of the early cars against the Turks in Tripolitania. They were quite effective, but not spectacularly so, and their first appearance did not have quite the same emotive appeal to the world's press as did the first tank action. Nevertheless, it was clear that their future was now assured and that they would prove a valuable addition to all armies, especially as the speed of mechanisation increased and the horsed soldier began to fade from the battlefield.

Daimler Panzerwagen, 1905. A modification of the four-wheel drive 1904 Daimler Panzerwagen, the world's first turreted armoured car, the 1905 model showed similarly good speed, range and mobility, and had heavier armament, but, although it was demonstrated to them, neither the Germans nor the Austrians saw the car's potential.

1 THE BEGINNINGS

Great Britain

Simms Motor Scout 1898. The first British development of a motorised vehicle for military use was Frederick R. Simms' 'Motor Scout', produced in 1898. It comprised a De Dion Bouton quadricycle powered by a $1\frac{1}{2}$ horsepower engine, with a Maxim machine gun and bullet-proof shield fitted in front of the handlebars.

Fowler B5 armoured tractor, 1900. This armoured steam traction engine was one of numerous types used for pulling trains of supplies during the Boer War. In order to protect the supply columns from raids by the Boers, armoured traction engines were ordered and four arrived in South Africa in July 1900. The B5s worked at Bloemfontein, Pretoria and Mafeking. There were loopholes in the armour, but no overhead cover. A field gun could be towed behind or hauled into the truck and carried.

Simms Motor War Car, 1902 (*Above left*). First demonstrated at the Crystal Palace, London on 4 April 1902, the Motor War Car had a boat-shaped body with rams fore and aft. It was built of 6 mm thick armour and mounted a pom-pom (Maxim 1-pdr quick firing gun) and two Maxim machine guns fitted with detachable shields. The normal crew was four, but it was claimed that 12 men could be carried if it was to be used as an armoured personnel carrier, a claim borne out by the photograph, although top hats were hardly the right headgear for fighting infantrymen! Its fully laden weight was $5\frac{1}{2}$ tons. Powered by a 16 hp Daimler engine with a four-speed gearbox, its top speed was 9 mph. The steel-tyred wheels restricted it to hard roads only.

Armstrong Whitworth, 1906 (*Above*). Designed by W G Wilson, one of the great pioneers of the first tanks, this car was built by Armstrong Whitworths of Newcastle-upon-Tyne. It had large wooden-spoked wheels, armour enclosing the engine and body (a side engine panel has been removed in the photograph). Armament was to be a 1-pdr pom-pom. Drums of steel cable and power take-off pulleys, with which the vehicle could pull itself out of heavy going, were mounted on either side of the body. It was 12 ft long, 5 ft wide and 5 ft high.

Armstrong Whitworth, 1913. There was a seven-year gap before Armstrong Whitworth followed up their earlier model, when they were invited to build an armoured car for Imperial Russia. Fully armoured, with a cylindrical turret which mounted a Maxim machine-gun, it saw service during World War 1. Note the crest on the side of the body, winged wheels, the symbol used by the Russians for motor-transport troops.

Ford Model T Machine Gun Car, 1913. A Model T Ford mounting a Vickers machine gun on the left of the driver, it had a low wooden body in which two men sat back to back with the driver and gunner.

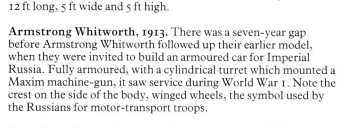

Austria

Daimler Panzerwagen, 1904. The first turreted armoured car in the world was this 1904 Daimler, with four-wheel drive, curved hull and dome-shaped turret, mounting a single water-cooled Maxim machine gun. The armour was about 3 mm thick which kept the weight down to under 3 tons. Top speed was 28 mph and its 35 hp engine had a good performance over a 155-mile radius of action. It was 13 ft long, 5 ft 11 ins wide and 8 ft 2 ins high.

Daimler Panzerwagen, 1905. In 1905, the Daimler Panzerwagen was modified by fitting a new turret, open at the rear, with two small openings in the front so that two Maxims could be fitted side by side. Demonstrated to the Germans during the Austro-Hungarian Army manoeuvres of 1905, it was surprisingly not adopted by either army.

France

Charron, Girardot et Voigt (CGV) Automitrailleuse, 1902. Built for the French Ministry of War and first exhibited at the Paris Motor Show in December 1902, this 40 hp chain-drive car was fitted with a circular tub-shaped armoured body in place of the rear seats. A Hotchkiss machine gun with a shield was pedestal-mounted in the tub, with all-round traverse. The armour was 6–7 mm thick.

CGV Automitrailleuse, 1904. This was the very first proper armoured car in France, with disc wheels, fully armoured body and a small rotating turret on the roof, mounting one Hotchkiss machine gun. The first was built in 1904. It weighed $3\frac{1}{4}$ tons and had a 30 hp engine. The improved models which appeared between 1906–08 weighed nearly $\frac{3}{4}$ ton less and had a more powerful (35 hp) engine. Some ten were sold to Russia. Note the troughs carried on the side to help cross obstacles. Tyres were self-sealing.

Char du Blessé Palisser, 1904. This early armoured ambulance had a box hull with a rounded roof, disc wheels and under-hull armour.

De Dion Bouton Anti-Aérienne, 1910 (*Below left*). The first French mobile anti-aircraft gun had a 75 mm AA gun mounted at the rear on a turntable. The bracing jacks are lowered in the firing position.

De Dion Bouton Anti-Aérienne, 1913 (*Below*). This was very similar to the earlier model, but eight-spoked wheels had replaced the artillery wheels, and a partial-faceted gunshield had been added.

Hotchkiss, 1909. This was the first armoured car to be built by Hotchkiss & Cie of St Denis, Seine and was similar to the early CGV. No protection was afforded to the driver or co-driver and the single Hotchkiss machine gun was mounted in the circular 'tub' behind, with a high shield. Four of these cars were sold to the Sultan of Turkey in 1909, but, when the Young Turkish Revolution broke out, the cars were taken over by the revolutionaries and used to overthrow the Sultan!

I THE BEGINNINGS

Germany

Opel Darracq, 1906. Based on a passenger car chassis, this had artillery wheels, horizontal radiator shutters, and flat, hinged armoured plates all round, with an open top and shutter ports for vision and weapons in the windscreen.

Ehrhardt Ballon Abwehr, 1906. This 5 cm anti-balloon cannon, with a low armoured hull and high rear turret, was first exhibited at the Berlin Motor Show of 1906. It was basically a standard truck chassis with chain-driven rear wheels. Its 60 hp petrol engine gave it a top speed of 29 mph. The BAK (Ballon Abwehr Kanone) weighed about 3 tons and had $3\frac{1}{2}$ mm thick armour. It carried 100 grenade and fragmentary shells on board. The 5 cm gun had a 60 degrees arc of traverse and elevation from -5 to $+70$ degrees.

Rheinmetall anti-balloon cannon truck, 1908. This semi-armoured 5 cm anti-balloon cannon truck was built by Rheinische Metallwaaren and Maschinenfabrik of Dusseldorf. One problem with this type was the difficulty of all-round traverse.

Daimler Platformwagen, 1910. In 1908, the Daimler Motor Company constructed a new platform truck, specially designed to mount an anti-balloon cannon. Krupp of Essen contributed their new 7.7 cm L/30, which was particularly suited to truck mounting. An improved version, with a more powerful engine, was produced two years later.

Daimler Platform Truck, 1911. Only one of the prototype trucks was produced. It mounted a 7.7 cm L/27 anti-balloon cannon.

Rheinmetall anti-balloon cannon truck, 1913. Rheinmetall produced this improved, four-wheel drive platform truck, which mounted a 7.7 cm L/27 anti-balloon cannon.

Italy

Isotta-Fraschini Tipo RM, 1911. The earliest Italian armoured car, with a conventional layout front engine, fully armoured hull and fully rotating turret. It weighed about 3 tons and had a top speed of 37 mph. In order to give it a better cross country performance, its solid rubber-tyred wheels were mounted in pairs at the rear, while those in front had steel flanges. Some saw service in North Africa in 1912 during the war with Turkey over Tripoli.

Fiat Arsenale, 1912. The large hull had a cylindrical turret, with one water-cooled machine gun, mounted about centre of the vehicle. Armoured and equipped by the Arsenale di Artigliera at Turin, the car had a small searchlight on top of the turret for night operations. The first Fiat armoured car, it was built towards the end of the Italo-Turkish war and was used in desert operations.

Bianchi (A), 1914 (*Below left*). Bianchi produced their first armoured car in 1912 (prototype), from which two models came two years later. The Model A had an open-top boxlike hull with no turret, and had pneumatic tyres. Note the wishbone wire-cutter which extended up over the entire hull and the pedestal-mounted machine gun.

Bianchi (B), 1914. This was very similar to the original prototype. It had a large cylindrical turret (dome-mounted), rounded radiator armour and disc wheels with solid tyres. Its dimensions were 14 ft 10 ins long, 5 ft 11 ins wide and 8 ft 3 ins high.

I THE BEGINNINGS
Russia

Russo-Balt, 1912. The first Russian-built armoured car was manufactured by Russo-Baltiskig Zavod (RBVZ) in Riga and saw service with the Automobile Corps. It mounted three machine guns (one front and one each side), and had disc wheels with no mudguards, a sloping radiator with a large access door hinged at the top, bevel-sided box hull and no turret.

1 THE BEGINNINGS
USA

Davidson Duryea, 1897. One of the earliest motor vehicles designed and built in the United States for military use. A .45 Colt Model 1895 automatic machine gun with armoured shield was mounted on a small commercial tricycle with a front steering wheel. It was designed by Col. Royal P. Davidson, the professor of tactics at the Military Academy, Wisconsin.

Davidson-Cadillac armored car, 1915 (*Below*). Col. Davidson also designed this 'Armoured Machine Gun Car'. It had a fully armoured hull, a small cupola, and disc wheels, and was powered by a 50 hp engine.

Davidson Duryea, 1898. This vehicle, also designed by Col. Davidson and replacing his unreliable 1897 tricycle, had a four-man crew, a rear-mounted three-cylinder engine, and a swivel-mounted .30 Colt Model 1895 machine gun.

Jeffery Quad armored truck, 1914. (*Bottom left*). The earliest of the completely armoured vehicles used by the USA was the Jeffery Quad, which had a louvred radiator, wheels in boxes and driver on the lefthand side. Note the armoured box over the driver's head and octagonal superstructure with flap openings.

Jeffery Armored Car No. 1, 1915. Based upon the Jeffery Quad trucks, this car had a rather clumsy topheavy design, with an open-topped turret in the centre and another on the lower rear deck, and weighed over 5½ tons. The ports in the turrets were for small arms rather than for mounted guns. The second version had protective boxes around the headlights.

2 The Great War

The opening stages of World War 1 were ideal for the use of armoured cars. The British, Belgians and, later, the French, all used them to considerable advantage for raiding missions and some reconnaissance, in those early days when the war was still fluid. The terrain in Belgium was perfect for armoured cars, with plenty of reasonable roads and few hilly areas. Patrols of Belgian soldiers armed with rifles and light machine guns used their improvised armoured cars to harry the invading German forces. The motor car thus proved extremely useful in this type of semi-guerilla role, putting into practice a theory which had been expounded during the Boer War by a British war correspondent for the use of armed motor cars carrying riflemen and a machine gun to raid against the Boers. The British also used their early armoured cars to defend forward airfields against German cavalry and to rescue the crews of shot-down aircraft. The first cars used in this role were part of a Royal Naval Air Squadron based in France, so the Royal Navy played a significant part in the history of early armoured cars, just as they were to do with tanks. Of all the armoured cars used in these early days the Rolls-Royce must stand out, its grace and performance making it a true thoroughbred.

Once the Western Front became static and warfare settled down to opposing lines of trenches with well-nigh impossible going between them, then the armoured car rather faded from the European battle scene, although the Russians did make use of them on more than one occasion to support an attack much in the same way as tanks were later employed. Armoured cars needed space and good going on which to operate, so it was left to individuals like Col. T. E. Lawrence to exploit their potential to the full, as he did so admirably during the British advance through Palestine. Another group of armoured cars, under Commander Locker Lampson, fought alongside the armies of the Czar of Russia and earned a considerable reputation. But these were perhaps only sideshows.

Even when the Western Front became more fluid, armoured cars were never used in large numbers. They did, however, have at least one opportunity to show what they might have achieved, and that was during the Battle of Amiens in 1918. A group of sixteen British armoured cars of the 17th Battalion, Tank Corps, managed to exploit a breakthrough, penetrate deep into enemy territory and play havoc in the rear areas, including shooting up an advanced Corps HQ. Sadly, such actions were all too rare, but did show what the speed and mobility of armoured cars could achieve in the right conditions.

Autocar, 1914. The US-built Autocar was employed successfully by the Canadians in France from 1915, notably during the German offensive on the Somme in March 1918, a point the photograph's original caption, dated 16 April 1918, makes in a manner characteristic of the period: 'Canadian Armoured Motor carrying machine guns. These cars did wonderful work during the Boche attack on the Somme. On the right is the front of the car, the driver's head and shoulders can just be seen.'

Great Britain

Rolls-Royce (first RNAS pattern). In September 1914, a Royal Naval Air Service (RNAS) wing, No. 1, commanded by Commander C. R. Samson, RN, and equipped with ten aircraft of various types, was based at Dunkirk with the task of locating and dealing with German airships en route to bomb London and southeast England. No. 1 Wing was also equipped with a number of touring motor cars and lorries, their job being to supplement air reconnaissance and rescue the crews of aircraft which were shot down. One of the cars, a Mercedes, was equipped with the only machine gun available, but very soon two more were borrowed from the French and fitted to other cars. The cars were also armoured locally after early encounters with German cavalry. The second car to be armoured was a Silver Ghost 'Alpine' Rolls-Royce 40/50 hp, seen here. The original armour was only boiler plate which would not stop rifle bullets under 500 yards, so Samson asked the Admiralty to supply proper armour plate from England, while they began to design a real armoured car.

Rolls-Royce (first Admiralty pattern), 1914. Following the reports sent by Commander Samson from France, the Admiralty Air Department designed proper armour to be fitted to some of the cars in Samson's squadron and this armour arrived in France during Autumn 1914. As the photograph shows, the armour was fairly basic in design, but it did provide full protection for the engine, sides and back, while the driver had overhead cover.

Wolseley (first Admiralty pattern), 1914. The other car for which the Admiralty produced armour plate was this 30/40 hp Wolseley. The radiator has a single door opening upwards instead of the double outward opening doors of the Rolls. Some slight protection was afforded to the front tyres by plates attached to the front of the mudguards. Neither of the Admiralty pattern designs was very popular in Samson's armoured car squadron because they gave little protection to the crew, apart from the driver.

Armoured AEC 'B' Type chassis, RNAS, 1914. In early September 1914, No. 1 Wing RNAS was reinforced by a detachment of 200 Royal Marines and it was decided to use them to provide support for the armoured car patrols. Twelve marines could be carried in this AEC lorry, the riflemen shooting through the loopholes whilst mounted. The armour was made locally by the same company who had provided the plating for the first armoured cars, Forges et Chantiers de France, of Dunkirk.

Talbot (first Admiralty pattern), 1914 (*Below left*). The main difference on the Talbot from the Rolls and Wolseley was the large rectangular armour plate in front of the radiator, although other models used in France and Belgium did have twin sideways opening armoured radiator doors.

Talbot (first Admiralty pattern) modified, 1914 (*Above*). In November 1914, a modified Talbot was produced, which had no rear wheel covers or separate driver's headcover. Instead, the armour around the entire crew compartment was built up to shoulder height. It sloped slightly inwards and had an open top. The armament was either two Maxim machine guns (as shown here), or one Maxim with a gunshield.

Auto-Carrier light car, 1914. Although the Army did not take over the RNAS armoured car squadrons until September 1915, there were a few experimental armoured cars built for the Army before that date. One was this light armoured car which used an AC chassis and was powered by a 4-cylinder 1500 cc engine. Note the large circular open-topped turret. No further cars were built, probably because the chassis, despite strengthening, was just not strong enough to take the armour.

23

AEC (LGOC Omnibus) 1914. This armoured car used a heavy commercial omnibus chassis, it was built by Woolwich Arsenal at the request of the War Office, and designed by an officer of the RNAS Armoured Car Force, who was engaged in experimental work. The armour was thick enough to stop rifle bullets at ranges of 100 yds and upwards.

Rolls-Royce (Admiralty pattern), 1914. The first three production cars were completed in early December 1914 and by mid-1915 six RNAS squadrons had been equipped with them. Their armament was a Vickers-Maxim machine gun. The 3½-ton Rolls was the most widely used armoured car of the Great War, seeing action in France, Egypt, the Dardanelles, East Africa and Russia. It was also used, of course, by Col. T. E. Lawrence in his famous campaigns in the Middle East. The car had a crew of three and a top speed of 50 mph. Its dimensions were 16 ft 7 ins long, 6 ft 3 ins wide and 7 ft 6 ins high.

Rolls-Royce 1914, modified for desert operations. In order to make life a little more bearable in desert conditions, the turret top and bevel plates were removed as shown in this photograph.

Rolls-Royce Experimental Car, 1915.
This experimental model had the turret
removed and a Vickers 1-pdr pom-pom
with an armoured shield fitted in its place,
but it was unsuccessful and was soon
discarded as there was insufficient
handling space. Note the very rudimentary
traverse.

Rolls-Royce Tender Car, 1914. This
splendid open roadster had low armour
plate only, with a Vickers machine gun
mounted at the rear on a low pedestal.

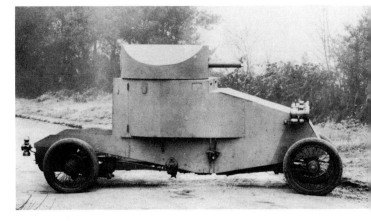

Lanchester, 1914. The prototype of the Lanchester had a very obviously bellied hull, a platform at the rear and a sloping front glacis plate over the engine. The turret was the same bevelled type as on the Rolls, mounting a single machine gun. Note the wire wheels without mudguards.

Lanchester, 1915. Production models which were built the following year were similar but did not belly downwards in the centre. Three RNAS squadrons were equipped with Lanchesters and went to France in 1915. The Russians were also supplied with the cars in 1915. Some 36 cars were also formed into a special squadron (known popularly as the Czar's British Squadron) and sent to help the Russian Imperial Government, under the command of Commander Locker-Lampson. They stayed in Russia until January 1918, two months after the Revolution began, when they were evacuated via Archangel. The 38 hp cars weighed about 5 tons, but had a top speed of 50 mph.

Delaunay-Belleville, 1915. As well as Rolls and Lanchesters there were a small number of Talbot and Delaunay-Belleville armoured cars. The latter had a large flat-topped turret containing a single Vickers-Maxim water-cooled machine gun. The armour from one of these cars was used on a Killen-Strait tractor in early tracked experiments in July 1915.

Sizaire-Berwick Wind-Wagon, 1915.
This was an interesting experiment tried
out at the RNAS Armoured Car Division
HQ at Wormwood Scrubs, during the
summer of 1915. A 110 hp Sunbeam
aircraft engine was used to power a four-
bladed propeller which was mounted upon
a Sizaire-Berwick chassis. The single
machine gun mounted by the driver was
only able to fire forward. It was never used
in action.

Talbot-Baxter, 1915. A Talbot 25 hp
chassis was used as the basis of an
armoured car for the 2nd King Edward's
Horse, which was a volunteer regiment
raised among colonials living in London, in
early 1915. It resembled the 1914 Rolls at
first glance, but had a distinctive
octagonal-shaped turret, mounting one
machine gun.

Isotta-Fraschini, 1915. Like the Talbot-
Baxter, this armoured car was built from
private funds for the Territorial Army. It
was an odd-looking vehicle with a long
sloping glacis plate and no turret, built on a
25 hp Isotta-Fraschini chassis.

Wolseley CP type, 1915. Two such armoured cars were built for the London Mounted Brigade and paid for by public subscription. It used a 30 cwt lorry chassis, with .196 in armour plate and a rotating turret mounting a single Vickers-Maxim machine gun. The War Office also ordered a similar car. Note the disc wheels with solid tyres.

Seabrook RNAS heavy armoured car, 1915. Some 25–30 of these 10-ton heavy armoured cars were built for use in support of the normal RNAS cars. Main armament was a 3-pdr gun and there were four machine gun mountings in addition, one in each corner of the open compartment. The chassis was a 5-ton Seabrook lorry, imported from the United States. Their weight did present problems although they did well in action around Ypres. Eventually, in May 1915, they were formed into heavy armoured squadrons of six cars each. A few cars saw service in the Western Frontier Force in Egypt, but proved unsuitable for desert work as they bogged down too easily in sand.

Jeffrey Quad, 1916. This four-wheel armoured car, built on the Jeffrey Quad chassis, was constructed in the USA in some quantity for the British Army. It was exactly the same as the Canadian Russell (page 32) with a single, rotating turret in the centre and four small semi-circular sponsons front and rear on each side of the body (each with two rifle ports). It weighed $6\frac{1}{2}$ tons, was powered by a 40 hp Buda engine and had a top speed of 20 mph on roads. They were used first in India in 1917 and after the Great War some saw service in Ireland. The armament of the original American models had been four machine guns, but those in British service had just one .303 in Vickers machine gun.

Pierce-Arrow anti-aircraft lorry, 1916. Pierce-Arrow heavy lorries imported from America were the basis of various armoured vehicles, like these armoured lorries, used to equip the Royal Marine Artillery AA Brigade. The cars mounted Vickers 2-pdr automatic pom-poms and saw service in France, where, between April 1915 and the end of 1917, they brought down about 20 enemy aircraft.

Peerless anti-aircraft lorry, 1916. The Peerless, which had very similar dimensions to the Pierce-Arrow anti-aircraft lorry but whose rear wheels had chain drive instead of shaft drive, was another American lorry used in the AA role.

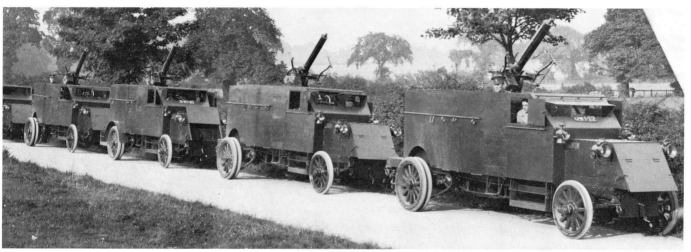

Pierce-Arrow (3-pdr), 1916. Specially built for Cdr Locker-Lampson's squadron, serving in Russia, were a number of heavy armoured cars, equipped with a 3-pdr naval gun, in a large turret at the rear, just forward of the back wheels. Their combat weight was over 9 tons which meant that their cross country performance was poor and they were rather top heavy. The engine armour is identical to that of the earlier AA lorries.

Ford (Admiralty pattern), 1917 (*Left*). This very light armoured car (its all up weight was just 21 cwts) was also built specially for Cdr Locker-Lampson's Russian squadron. The car had an open rear, with a Vickers machine gun on a tripod, although at least one car was modified with a shorter body and fitted with a Lewis gun.

Sheffield-Simplex, 1916 (*Above*). A number of these cars were specially designed and built for the Russian Imperial Army in 1916. The car had twin turrets each mounting a Vickers-Maxim machine gun, weighed about 5 tons and was powered by a 30 hp engine. The tyres were self-sealing.

Austin, 1915. More Austin armoured cars were built during the Great War than any other type, most being destined for the Russian Imperial Army. The first model, pictured here, had a tall cab with sloping sides and twin parallel turrets, each mounting a single machine gun.

Austin (second type), 1915. Variations with this model included a lower cab with vertical sides, ventilator domes on the turrets and a small platform at the rear of the hull. They were also sold to Russia, deliveries being stopped when the Revolution began.

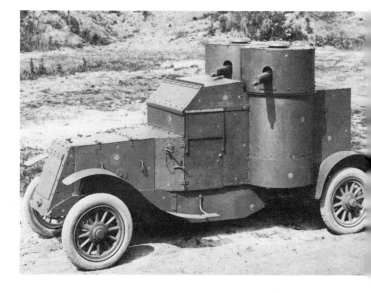

Austin (final pattern), 1918. Dual rear wheels were fitted on the final model, and although not visible in this photograph, a separate steering wheel was added for use when driving backwards. Some modifications were necessary to the rear armour to enable the second driver to see where he was going! Small wing plates were added on either side of the machine gun openings to help to protect the gun barrels. The car had a top speed of 35 mph and a crew of five, and its dimensions were 16 ft long, 6 ft 7 ins wide and 7 ft 10 ins high.

Anti-aircraft lorry, 13-pdr. Although not strictly an armoured fighting vehicle this motor lorry mounted a 13-pdr (9 cwt) quick firing anti-aircraft gun on a pedestal mount. This particular gun was photographed in action on the outskirts of Armentieres in March 1916.

Peerless anti-aircraft lorry, 3-in. A pedestal-mounted AA 3-in gun, larger than a 13-pdr, was the armament of this drop-side Peerless lorry.

2 THE GREAT WAR
Commonwealth

Australia: Ford Patrol Car, 1916. An open Ford Model T car, unarmoured but equipped with a machine gun, was used as a patrol car by the Australians.

Canada: Autocar, 1914. Twenty of these open-topped cars were purchased from the United States to equip a motor machine gun regiment, the brain child of Raymond Brutinel, a former French officer then living in Canada. Arriving in the UK in October 1914, they reached France in early 1915 and did much good work, in particular during the German offensive in March 1918. Their twin Vickers water-cooled machine guns provided a valuable mobile reserve of firepower. Note the solid tyres and armoured plate (about $\frac{3}{4}$ in thick).

Canada: Russell armoured truck, 1915. Identical to the American Jeffrey with duplicate driving controls front and rear, and also large wire-cutter hooks. They were probably assembled in Canada after being imported from the USA.

India: Cadillac (India pattern) armoured car, 1915. Bristling with rifles and machine guns, the car had an armoured hull with a gabled roof built onto a Cadillac car and was based in Calcutta where it was used for internal security duties.

India: Fiat armoured car, 1915. There were various armoured cars in India, built on Fiat car and lorry chassis. The photograph shows the Fiat War Office Design of 1915, which was adapted from the AEC which it strongly resembles (see previous section, page 24). Note the built-out driver's cab, hatches in sides and disc wheels. This armoured car used a $1\frac{1}{2}$-ton Fiat lorry chassis and the armoured plate was supplied from England.

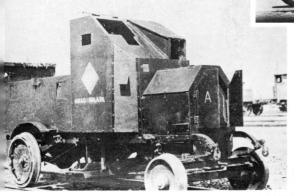

India: Fiat armoured car converted for rail use. An interesting adaptation of the Fiat War Office Design, for use on the railway tracks.

India: Rolls-Royce armoured car, 1915. This particular armoured car was No. 2641 and started life as a standard Silver Ghost 40/50 hp, built in 1911. The Rajah of Ticca presented it to the Government at the start of the Great War, and it was fitted with an improvised armoured body and took part in both internal security and frontier security operations.

India: Rolls-Royce armoured car, 1919. At the end of 1919, car No. 2641 was fitted with a new armoured body which had been designed by 1st Armoured Motor Brigade and built in the Gun Carriage Factory at Jubbulpore. In 1920 it was used as the bridal carriage at the wedding of the adjutant of 1st Brigade and thus acquired the name *Wedding Bells*. It saw service for many years right up to World War 2.

India: Standard 1916. The first armoured car to be completed at Lilloah was this Standard, not unlike the early Rolls, but with higher sides, providing the machine gun crew with more cover.

India: Standard with wire cutters, 1916. Interesting addition to this Standard armoured car was a pair of wire cutters, covering the entire frontal area of the car. An Indian Armed Forces number plate and arrow are on the bonnet side.

India: Willys, 1916. The striking dome-shaped turret atop the box-shaped hull was built by the East India Railway Shops onto this Willys utility car. It also had double wire cutter rails, solid tyres and disc wheels.

Austria

Romfell armoured car, 1915. During World War 1, the Austrian Army formed a small number of armoured car units, but used mainly captured enemy cars (Italian and Russian). There were, however, two Austrian-built cars, the first of these being the Romfell, which had a distinctive inward-sloping body, circular turret, bevelled all round and mounting a machine gun. Note also the disc wheels and solid tyres.

Juncoviz I armoured car, 1915. This was the other home produced Austrian armoured car, using an Austro-Fiat chassis, with a built-up armoured body which had ports for machine guns in front and sides.

Juncoviz II armoured car. The later model of the Juncoviz was very similar in design to the Juncoviz I, but the armour plate extended much lower all round, with the rear sections hinged so as to allow access to the rear wheels.

Belgium

Improvised armoured car, 1914. One of the many passenger cars and lorries pressed into service by the Belgians to counter the German invasion in 1914, was this touring car, which had a single Lewis gun mounted on a pedestal. Such cars were also used to carry sharpshooters in raids against the advancing Germans, but clearly suffered from lack of armoured protection.

Minerva armoured car, 1914. The armour plate designed for the Minerva was basic but effective, an open topped crew compartment containing a single Hotchkiss machine gun with or without a shield. Later models mounted a 37 mm cannon. This photograph of an early Minerva was taken in November 1914.

Minerva, streamlined version. This later model of the Minerva had a more streamlined appearance, with curved shields over the driver and co-driver, plus a half-dome turret at the rear and covers over the rear wheels.

Minerva armoured car. A slight modification to the 1914 model Minerva was to round the hull armour both at the rear and front. The photograph shows an aggressive group of 'sharpshooters' and their supporting Minerva armoured car.

Mors improvised armoured car, 1914.
The Mors passenger car, like the Minerva, was used as an armoured car, with steel plates fastened to the body and doors. Note also the plate hanging down at the rear to protect the tyres.

Autocanon Mors, 1915. The Autocanon Mors had more armour plate than the Minerva, the hull being high enough to protect the crew even when they were standing. The main armament was a 37 mm cannon, with an armour shield. Note also the Hotchkiss machine gun mounted above it, one of the earliest examples of mounting a coaxial machine gun. The engine gave 20 hp. A squadron of Belgian armoured cars (mainly Mors) was sent to Russia in early 1916. Next to the Mors Autocanon in the photograph is a Mors semi-armoured observation and command vehicle.

Peugeot armoured car, 1915.
Supplementing the Autocanon Mors in the 'Corps des Autos-Canons-Mitrailleuses Russie' were a number of French Peugeots, which were very similar except that they had no armoured protection on their engines and no gunshield on their 37 mm cannons. Wheels were the same as on the Mors (note that they are double at the rear because of the extra weight of the armour plate). The squadron saw plenty of action and earned high praise from the Tsar.

SAVA armoured car, 1914 (*Below far left*).
Another excellent armoured car produced by the Belgians was the Automitrailleuse SAVA, the initials standing for 'Societé Anversoise pour Fabrication de Voitures Automobiles' of Antwerp, which had been founded before the Great War. Engine and crew compartments were fully protected and the Hotchkiss machine gun was contained in a dome shaped turret, open at the rear. Note also the side access doors below the turret and the large spotlight used to supplement the powerful headlamps in night operations.

De Dion armoured lorry, 1914 (*Left*).
One of a number of light lorries to be given improvised armour was this De Dion, the plating being curved up over the driver to protect him. A 37 mm cannon was mounted on a pedestal in the rear.

2 THE GREAT WAR
France

Peugeot, 1914 (*Above right*). This early French armoured car had armour all round, a machine gun with shield, and artillery wheels. It was one of a number of improvised armoured cars which appeared on various chassis early in the war. However, when the Western Front settled down to trench warfare, the need for armoured cars diminished.

Peugeot, 1916 (*Right*). In 1916, the Peugeot company used their standard 18 hp touring car chassis and fitted twin rear wheels. On to this was built an armoured body with a small turret.

Renault Autoblindée, 1915 (*Below*). An early French armoured car was this Renault, with full armour plate, a sloping front bonnet and a single machine gun with shield in the open rear of the car.

Renault Autoblindée, 1915. Very similar to the last model, this one had more armour plate around the body, but not, surprisingly, around the engine. It mounted a machine gun in an open rear shield or a very wide wedge-shaped shield, open at the rear. The latter type can be seen leading this mixed column of armoured cars.

Renault Autocanon 37 mm, 1915. This was the other version of the Renault that appeared in early 1915, mounting a 37 mm cannon in a wedge-shaped shield, at the rear of the car. Renault built many cars, even before the outbreak of World War 1, so they were clear favourites to be armoured, but one source estimates that only 39 Renault armoured cars of all types survived the war, so casualties must have been high. This photograph was taken on the Western Front in 1917. The cannon was primarily for AA use.

Renault armoured personnel carrier, 1916. Taken at the Renault factory, this is the same model as seen earlier, but without the machine gun, although the post mount remains. It could be used in this form for carrying the sharpshooters.

Automitrailleuse White, 1915. Some 20 of these armoured cars were constructed from White trucks imported from USA. With lefthand drive, and conventional appearance, this 35 hp car had a top speed of 28 mph and a radius of action around 150 miles. It had a crew of four, and a main armament of one 37 mm gun plus one Hotchkiss machine gun, or two machine guns.

White Laffly, 1918. Accounting for the majority of those French armoured cars which survived the war, some remaining in service until 1940, a total of 230 Automitrailleuse White Laffly 1918 was built. These 6-ton cars were similar to the earlier Automitrailleuse White of 1915, but had right not lefthand drive. The photograph gives a good view of the 37 mm cannon and Hotchkiss machine gun.

Renault Autocanon des Fusiliers Marins, 1916. Manned by French naval personnel, these guns were used as mobile artillery rather in the same way as the earlier British Seabrook RNAS heavy armoured cars had been used by Commander Samson's unit. This time the gun was the French Autocanon 47 mm, fully armoured and mounted on the rear of a Renault lorry chassis with solid tyred artillery wheels. It could only fire rearwards.

Autocanon de 155, 1916. This is an example of a heavier type of field gun, a 155 mm howitzer, mounted upon an unarmoured lorry chassis.

Germany

Daimler MG Wagen, 1914. After an earlier prototype, based upon a Daimler passenger car, this model used a lorry chassis, with twin rear-facing Maxim machine guns. Note the gun crew's seats facing one another.

Bussing Panzerkraftwagen, 1915. The Germans had no armoured cars in service at the start of the Great War but rapidly noted the Belgians highly successful use of them. The three main motor manufacturing companies, Daimler, Bussing and Ehrhardt, were each told to build an armoured car. Bussing built a large car some 31 ft long with armour 7 mm thick. The engine was a 90 hp Bussing. Three Maxim machine guns carried inside could be used in no less than ten different positions – six in the hull, four in the turret. Note also the externally-mounted presumably AA, machine guns. Here, foliage camouflages the car.

Daimler Panzerkraftwagen, 1915. Daimler's contender, also large, had a box-shaped hull mounting a big cylindrical turret which had four ports around it, each with shutter doors. Similar ports were located on the hull sides (two each), front and rear. Three Maxim machine guns were normally carried. It had a crew of eight or nine and an 80 hp engine. Note the extended rims on the front wheels.

Panzerkraftwagen Ehrhardt, 1915.
The third prototype armoured car
produced at the beginning of World War 1
was the Ehrhardt which had a front
mounted engine and four-wheel drive. It
was of similar design to the Daimler and
Bussing prototypes, with a large body and
a cylindrical turret. There were again
numerous ports with shutters, through
which the complement of three machine
guns could be fired. The engine was
capable of producing 85 hp. The crew was
ten men.

Panzerkraftwagen Ehrhardt, 1917.
This later model was very similar to the
1915 prototype, except for the extended
rims on the front wheels, and armoured
boxes around the headlamps and over the
rear wheels, for added protection.

Captured armoured cars in German use. The Germans supplemented their small number of home-produced armoured cars with captured Allied equipment, with which they equipped their armoured car units, as this interesting group of photographs shows.

Left. The crew of an Austin captured from the Russians, posing proudly with their mascot on top of the car.

Below. This photograph contains both an Italian Fiat, on the left, and another Austin on the right.

Bottom left. This photograph shows a complete German armoured car unit, containing both captured Italian and Russian armoured cars.

Daimler Motor Vehicle 14 with L/27 anti-balloon cannon. Daimler's 1914 platform truck, designated Motor Vehicle 14, and mounting a 7.7 cm L/27 anti-balloon cannon, was the standard German motorised anti-aircraft artillery during the Great War.

Italy

Autoblindata Lancia IZ, 1915. Based on the Lancia IZ light truck chassis, this 4-ton armoured car quickly became the standard Italian armoured car of World War 1 and went on to be used in the Italian colonies right up to World War 2. This early model has an unusual turret arrangement with one small turret containing a single machine gun mounted on top of a larger turret with two machine guns. With a speed of some 35 mph and a radius of action of 250 miles, the large roomy hull had plenty of space for its six-man crew. Note also the wire cutters.

Autoblindata Lancia IZM (Ansaldo AB), 1917. The later model of the Lancia disposed of the early model's little top turret, and, instead, the third machine gun was ball mounted at the rear of the hull. The machine guns were all St Etienne and some 25,000 rounds of ammunition were carried in each car.

Ante Aerea 102/35, 1917 (*Above and right*). This mounted a 10.2 cm anti-aircraft gun on a Lancia IZ truck. The rest of the gun team, ammunition and long split trails, had to be carried on other similar vehicles, as the photograph at the right shows.

Russia

Pierce-Arrow heavy armoured car (rebuilt). The RNAS unit in Russia (Cdr Locker Lampson's squadron) had a number of Pierce-Arrow heavy armoured cars mounting 3-pdr guns. Some were captured by the Bolsheviks and later rebuilt in Petrograd where they were rearmed with 57 mm guns.

Putliov-Garford armoured car, 1914. In 1914, a heavy armoured car was built at the Putliov works in Petrograd. It weighed 11 tons and was based upon an American Garford chassis. It had two side sponsons with machine guns and a large turret at the rear which mounted another machine gun and the main armament – a 57 mm or 76.2 mm assault gun. There was also a strange-looking armoured chute which protected the barrel of the main gun. Unfortunately, it was top-heavy and in consequence had a poor performance, although a number were adapted to run along railway lines, It was among the most long-lived of all Russian armoured cars.

Peerless armoured car, 1914. Like the Putliov-Garford armoured car, this was used in Russia in 1914. It had a small cylindrical turret mounted on top of a truck chassis with a box-like hull, armoured over the engine. There was a 7.62 mm Vickers-Maxim machine gun in the turret and one on either side and one at the rear of the hull. The Peerless weighed $7\frac{1}{2}$ tons and had a crew of five.

Benz-Megbrov armoured car, 1916. Designed by a Russian captain of cavalry, Megbrov, who was killed in action only days after its completion, this armoured car was built on a German Benz chassis with rounded armoured bonnet, plus twin turrets mounted diagonally, which was the favourite arrangement for Russian armoured cars. No quantity production of this model was undertaken, but an earlier Renault-Megbrov car (designed in 1915) was produced in quantity and looked very similar. This example has fallen into German hands.

Lasky-Ehrhardt armoured car, 1915.
The basis was a German passenger car, armoured and with a small cylindrical turret. The artillery wheels had glycerine-filled pneumatic tyres. Note the long, sloping armoured bonnet.

Austin armoured car. As explained in the British section, various models of the Austin armoured car were produced by the UK and sold to Russia. Here is a typical example of an Austin, seen in Galicia in 1918.

Poplavko-Jeffrey AB-9 armoured car 1917 (*Below left*). Designed, like the Benz-Megbrov, by a Russian officer, Staff Captain Poplavko this car used a four-wheel drive Jeffrey Quad lorry and weighed some 8 tons. It had a five-man crew and thick armour – up to 16 mm. It was armed with two machine guns and was powered by two engines. It was, perhaps, a follow-up to another Poplavko-designed armoured car on a Jeffrey chassis, which had been produced two years earlier. Two AB-9s are seen here to the right of an Austin armoured car.

White armoured car, 1915 (*Below right*). This was based upon an American passenger car. It was fitted with artillery wheels (solid tyres) and had armour very similar to that of an Austin.

Fiat armoured car, 1915 (*Left*). These were originally built for France using an American chassis, then armoured with the usual Russian double turret arranged diagonally, so that it closely resembles the Austin and various other cars. Note the artillery wheels with glycerine filled pneumatic tyres – an *ad hoc* method of self-sealing. This Fiat has been taken over by revolutionaries at the storming of the Winter Palace in 1917.

Gulikevich half-tracked armoured car, 1915 (*Top right*). Designed by an engineer called Colonel Gulikevich, the prototype of this semi-tracked armoured car was produced in 1915 using an imported American Lombard artillery tractor which was then armoured at the Putilov works.

Gulikevich half-tracked armoured car, 1917 (*Centre right*). The Gulikevich system was applied to a number of other armoured cars. Here one is used for anti-riot operations in a Russian town. They also proved to be much better in mud and snow than ordinary wheeled armoured cars.

Ad hoc Fiat armoured car, 1917 (*Above*). This unusual photograph was taken in Galicia and shows what appears to be the cab and armament (a Maxim water-cooled machine gun with shield) of a Ford (Admiralty pattern) armoured car, which has been put into the back of a Fiat lorry. The car was probably used by the RNAS armoured car unit, when it was operating in support of the Russian 2nd Cavalry Division in Galicia.

Austin-Putilov half-tracked armoured car, 1916 (*Bottom right*). An even more successful half-track than the Gulikevich was designed by the technical manager of the Tsar's garage in Petrograd, which had its origins in work he had done trying to improve the performance of some of the Tsar's motor cars in snow. He was a Frenchman, Adolphe Kegresse, and his system was applied to Austin cars. In addition to light tracks replacing the rear wheels, there were two arms on the front of the car each carrying a roller, to assist in obstacle crossing. Of the original 60 ordered, very few were completed before the revolution began in 1917. However, 60 were later completed for the new Red Army on both Austin and Packard chassis.

USA

White armored car No. 2, 1915. The White Motor Company designed and built this armoured car using a 1½-ton White commercial truck. At over 4 tons, it was heavy for its size (14 ft 4 ins long), and the drive was only to the rear wheels. However, the 36 hp engine gave it a potential top speed of 40 mph. Note the large cylindrical turret.

King armored car, 1916 (*Left*). One of the lightest American armoured cars of World War 1 was the King, built by the Armored Motor Company of Detroit. It weighed only 5,280 lbs, had a turret very similar to early British cars, bevelled, and mounting a .30 Benet-Mercier machine gun. The car carried two planks which acted as fenders and also as unditching planks. Dual rear wheels helped its cross-country performance. It was bought by both the Army and the US Marine Corps. Its top speed was 45 mph.

King armored car USMC version (*Above*). The USMC version of the King had a sloping rear, a different turret, $\frac{3}{16}$ in armoured plate and a top speed of some 45 mph. Later models had solid tyres and wooden-spoked wheels instead of the wire wheels and pneumatic tyres seen here. The car in this photograph has had its engine armour removed.

Mack armored car, 1916. Constructed by the International Motor Company of New York and based upon the Mack 2-ton truck, it weighed 4½ tons, and normally mounted two Colt machine guns with curved shields. The tyres were made of solid rubber blocks. The Mack was 19⅔ ft long and 6½ ft wide.

Mack armored car, second model. The original model Mack had poor engine cooling so the front was altered to include cooling slots, as seen on the example here (right), pictured during a parade in New York with a Locomobile.

Locomobile armored car, 1916. Another big, heavy armoured car was built on the Locomobile chassis and is seen here on the left of a Mack. They were used by the 1st Field Artillery Battalion, New York National Guard.

M1918 armored car, 1918 (*Below*). This wooden mock-up on a White chassis had two seven-sided turrets and was designed to protect the lines of communication in France. The Services and Supply element of the American Expeditionary Force had asked for 150 of these cars, but General Pershing did not approve and only this mock-up was built. The turrets faced fore and aft.

White armored car, 1918. This was White's successor to their armored car No. 2 and was built by the Van Dorn Ironworks of Cleveland in 1918. It had a smaller turret, weighed less than its predecessor and was built of $\frac{1}{4}$ in plate. No armament was ever mounted and the cars never left the USA.

Armored Observation Automobile, 1917. Sometimes referred to as the Clark Observation Car after the man who built the tower, this strange looking device comprised a streamlined, torpedo-shaped car (probably a Pierce-Arrow), with an 18 ft tower attached. What a target!

3 Between The Wars

Between the world wars, armoured cars showed their value on some very strange battlefields and under very different conditions to those they had faced during World War 1. They were mainly used for a variety of internal security tasks and policing duties. Compared with tanks they were economical to operate, easier to move around, more reliable mechanically, and far simpler to maintain. They could move quickly and bring firepower to bear more effectively than much larger formations of either infantry or cavalry, while the appearance of a single armoured car could have a considerable sobering effect upon a riotous situation. The nations with colonial empires such as Great Britain, France and Italy, all made good use of their armoured cars in the internal security and policing roles. In Britain, some new cars were built to carry out these tasks, but for the most part it was a matter of using up old wartime stocks until new cars could be designed.

The departure of the horse from the battlefield was now only a matter of time. As the cavalry of all nations moved towards mechanisation, some more rapidly than others, so some changed their horses for armoured cars, while others chose light tanks. It has always been a difficult business to chose between the light tank and the armoured car, both having their obvious advantages and disadvantages. The British tended to prefer the former, while the Germans were more or less forced towards the latter, because they were the only type of AFV allowed under the Treaty of Versailles. Even when the Germans threw aside all pretence and started full-scale rearmament in the mid-1930s, they still continued to build large numbers of armoured cars, which were to prove their usefulness as they developed their *Blitzkrieg* tactics.

Smaller nations also began to build their own armoured cars, having first bought from the larger producers in order to learn the art. The Czechs and Swedes both produced highly successful models which they then sold for export. Armoured cars were ideal, relatively cheap training vehicles for expanding armoured forces, and the advent of better and better radio communications extended their range and versatility. The Germans, Italians and Russians all sent 'volunteers' to fight in the Spanish Civil War and used Spain to try out their new vehicles and equipment.

It would be true to say that the major step forward in armoured car evolution that took place between the wars, was the actual design and building of these valuable AFVs from scratch. No longer was it merely a matter of adapting a civilian car or lorry chassis to take armour plate and some form of armament. If the cars were to operate properly, then they had to be designed and built from scratch. Not only did this mean that the designers were free to examine a wide variety of means of improving cross-country performance, but they could also incorporate features which the civilian vehicles had never required, such as the ability to drive in either direction without loss of vision, speed or steering. Four-wheel drive became the 'norm', while protection and general crew conditions were greatly improved.

However, it must be said that interest in armoured cars remained patchy right up to the outbreak of World War 2. Great Britain in the 1930s, for instance, provides a good example of this lack of positive commitment. Pre-war plans allowed for only one armoured car regiment with under 40 armoured cars on its establishment, as the *total* armoured car force available to the British Expeditionary Force. It would take the disasters of 1940 to reawaken British interest in the armoured car.

BA-27, 1927. The first Russian armoured car to appear after World War 1 was the BA-27, following the First Five-Year Plan of 1927. Here, one of the crew cleans a BA-27's 37 mm tank gun. The heavy rivetted armour is evident.

3 BETWEEN THE WARS
Great Britain

Peerless armoured car, 1919. Postwar problems in Ireland and the Empire meant that the British Army had a continuing requirement for armoured cars for use on internal security duties and the like. Most of the wartime cars were almost worn out, so new ones had to be built. The first, the Peerless 1919 pattern, was a Peerless lorry chassis onto which was fitted an armoured hull and double turret assembly very similar to that of the final pattern of the wartime Austin armoured cars. In fact, Austins did the work, beginning in late 1919. Some of the first cars completed were sent to Ireland in 1920. The Derbyshire Yeomanry still had one of the robust old cars as late as 1940. Weighing 5.8 tons, it had 8 mm armour, a crew of four and a top speed of 18 mph. It mounted two Hotchkiss machine guns.

Peerless armoured lorry. This armoured lorry was used during IS operations as a troop carrying vehicle with anti-grenade netting over the top. However, it is surprising to see that the engine was not armoured.

Rolls-Royce armoured car, 1920. Very similar to the wartime 1914 pattern, the 3.8-ton 40–50 hp Rolls-Royce had disc-type wheels instead of wire spokes, and a slightly higher turret. There were louvres fitted to the armoured doors on the radiator. The armament of this 45 mph car was a single Vickers machine gun. This car can be seen in the Tank Museum, Bovington Camp.

Car, Armoured Rolls-Royce Type A. As well as the Army the RAF used the 1920 pattern, as seen here, but the Air Ministry contract was entirely separate from the War Office contract. They were used to equip RAF Armoured Car Companies for service in Iraq and Egypt.

Car, Rolls-Royce Type A Armed Tender. Another RAF type, this had a lorry body, sometimes with a machine gun mounted in the rear. It was also used as a desert track marker with a pointed, hinged spade fixed in the rear.

Car, Armoured Rolls-Royce Type A modified (*Below*). Experience in desert conditions led the RAF to dispense with the balloon tyres originally fitted to the Type A and to fit heavier commercial pattern wheels, with large section tyres, as seen here.

Rolls-Royce IP (India Pattern) prototype (*Above*). The Government of India decided soon after the war to place orders for armoured cars to be built to their own specifications. One of the first was the India Pattern Rolls and the photograph shows the prototype for this model. Note the larger hull, and the domed turret, fitted with ports for extra machine guns. Inside, the hull was lined with woven asbestos in order to make it cooler. The tyres were solid rubber.

Rolls-Royce IP, 1921 (*Left*). The first IP model had two front and two rear ball-mounted Vickers in a dome-shaped turret. Only two were usually carried each with 5,000 rounds. A full company (16 cars) was equipped; some were also built for Persia.

Rolls-Royce armoured car, 1924. Although the bodywork clearly resembled that of the 1920 model, the 1924 Rolls had some major design changes, the most noticeable being the new turret, with a cupola for the commander. The Vickers machine gun was now in a spherical mounting. The car weighed 4½ tons. At 16 ft 2 ins, it was 5 ins shorter than the 1920 pattern, but was slightly wider and taller, 6 ft 4 ins and 8 ft 4 ins. The crew remained at three. The speed (45 mph) and radius of action (180 miles) were unchanged.

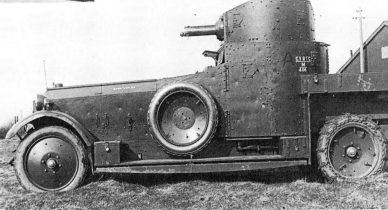

Lancia armoured car, 1919. When the RAF decided to go for their own armoured cars, Lancias were among the first to be ordered. Lancias also saw action in Ireland, where they were used by the police up to 1922. The original model, seen here, was more an armoured personnel carrier than an armoured car, as it had no vehicle-mounted weapon, relying on those of the occupants. Wire netting was often added to the roof on IS duty. Later, some Lancias were handed over to the Irish Government and these then had armoured roofs added and were normally equipped with Lewis machine guns. Apart from the front shutter, Lancias had no bonnet armour.

Lancia armoured car, turreted pattern 1922. The other RAF Lancia had a slightly different body design which fully enclosed the vehicle, and also had a small multi-sided turret mounting a single Lewis gun. Lancia armoured cars saw service with the RAF throughout the period from 1922 to the early 1930s, when they were replaced by Rolls cars.

Crossley armoured personnel carrier. Typical of some of the early postwar attempts to produce bulletproof cars and lorries for use in Ireland was this Crossley, which had armoured plates fitted onto the sides. A grenade screen was sometimes added on top.

Crossley armoured car, India Pattern 1923. The second batch of cars after the Rolls to be specially built for the Indian Government were based upon the cheaper Crossley chassis. These began with the 1923 pattern, which had a 50 hp engine and, on some cars, the ability to electrify the outside of the hull – most useful when dealing with riotous crowds!

Crossley armoured car, India Pattern 1925. Various modifications were introduced on different Crossley models. The 1925 pattern, for example, had more engine air louvres and a different arrangement for carrying the unditching planks on the sides. Two similar cars were supplied to South Africa.

Chevrolet armoured car, India Pattern 1939. By 1939, the chassis of the Indian Pattern Rolls-Royce and Crossley armoured cars were worn out, so their armoured hulls were removed and fitted onto Chevrolet truck chassis, which had dual rear wheels and pneumatic tyres that gave a much better ride. They saw service during World War 2.

Leyland armoured car, 1922 (*Far left*). Seen here leaving the factory, this was an updated version of the Leyland S3 produced during World War 1, but it had a different chassis and radiator shutter (one instead of two). The same ten-sided conical turret was mounted on top of the high hull.

Morris ad hoc armoured car, 1927 (*Left*). An interesting photograph of a locally produced armoured car, built on to a Morris truck chassis. It was used by the Volunteer Force in Singapore in 1927. Note the 6 × 4 chassis and huge, round turret with front bevel mounting a single machine gun.

Armstrong-Siddeley-Pavesi, 1929. This odd looking big-wheeled, articulated tractor was used both for towing artillery guns and as a machine gun carrier. In the latter role it had no armour, but mounted a single Vickers machine gun alongside the driver. The wheels were 4 ft 3 ins in diameter.

Alvis-Straussler armoured car 3D, 1937 (*Below left*). This 4-ton armoured car was one of a series of armoured cars designed by Nicholas Straussler (see page 88), a Hungarian engineer, who is probably best remembered for his invention of the Duplex Drive (DD) System as a means of making a conventional tank swim. Note the multi-faceted turret, with one machine gun; there was another machine gun in the hull alongside the driver. There was a second set of driving controls in the rear. A number of these cars were delivered to the Dutch East Indies, and others to the Portuguese Army.

Alvis-Straussler armoured car Type A, 1938 (*Above*). Built to RAF requirements, this model had only one machine gun in the turret. Note the driver's cowls at front and rear. They saw service in Aden with the RAF Armoured Car Unit.

Austro-Daimler Baby. Very similar to the ADSK Kleinerpanzerwagen (see later in Austrian section, page 67), the 'Baby' had a somewhat larger hull. A modified version was produced later still – the Steyr-Daimler-Puch/Morris.

Steyr armoured car, 1938. Another experimental model was this Austro-Daimler/Morris, which had a Morris engine. Its turret was very similar to the one on the Guy armoured car (see later in World War 2 section, page 135). It was tested in 1938 as a rival design to the Guy, but not adopted.

Barbette carriage Mk 1, 1930. Mounted on a Ford chassis, this car had an armoured cab and bonnet, with an entirely separate revolving, box-shaped turret containing a 2-pdr gun. There was another model produced in mock-up form only, which had a slope-sided box hull with the gun firing to the rear.

**Morris experimental armoured car,
1935** (*Right and far right*). Between 1935
and 1936 Morris Motors Ltd designed an
experimental armoured car which
appeared in various guises. The first had a
large cylindrical turret which could be
raised and lowered, as the photographs
show. It was based upon the chassis of the
15 cwt Morris Commercial truck which
was the standard vehicle of its class in
service use. It weighed 4.2 tons (laden) and
had a special engine fitted by Morris.

**Morris experimental anti-tank car,
1935.** The next experimental Morris model
differed from the first in having no turret.
Instead, a Boys anti-tank rifle and a Bren
.303 in machine gun were mounted behind
a semi-circular shield. The armour profile
around the driver's position has also been
altered.

**Morris experimental armoured car,
1936** (*Below*). Yet a third experimental
model based on the same chassis, this car
had a fully traversing turret similar to that
of the contemporary light tank, complete
with cupola and single Vickers .50 machine
gun. It weighed 3.882 tons (laden), was
powered by Morris Commercial 25 hp
engine with normal transmission and four-
speed gearbox. Note the interesting
'dazzle' camouflage.

Morris experimental reconnaissance car, 1936. The fourth and final experimental model had a body about 18 ins longer than the others, a different air scoop on the front of the radiator, and a smoke discharger mounted in between the Boys and Bren in the open-topped turret. It was the one finally chosen for production as the armoured car reconnaissance Morris Model CS9/LAC.

Morris armoured reconnaissance Model CS9/LAC (*Below left*). The photograph shows the production model of the CS9, with no armament fitted. Note the different shape to the final turret. One hundred were ordered and some were later converted into armoured command vehicles. They were still in service at the start of World War 2, the BEF armoured car regiment (12th Lancers), for example, taking them to France in 1939. Others were used in the Libyan campaign as command cars by 11th Hussars. The production model weighed 4.2 tons, had a crew of four, a top speed of 45 mph and a range of 240 miles.

Straussler armoured car AC1, 1933 (*Below*). This was the first of the Straussler armoured cars mentioned on page 56. It was built in Hungary and brought to the UK. Note the symmetrical hull and mounting for a centrally placed turret which was never installed.

Straussler armoured car AC2, 1935 (*Left and far left*). Also built in Hungary and brought to Britain, the improved version of the AC1, the AC2 had four-wheel steering, and a single machine gun in the turret. The photographs show off its very symmetrical shape.

Vickers wheel-cum-track. Although space does not permit the coverage of all wheel-cum-tracks, this photograph and the following one do show early attempts at using the wheel and track on the same vehicle in an 'either/or' situation.

Vickers-Wolseley wheel-cum-track. Known also as the armoured car D4E1, this wheel-cum-track had the ability to run on either type of locomotion, so in its form shown here it was definitely an armoured car. Note the large dome-shaped turret mounting a single machine gun. Built in 1927, it was based on the standard Wolseley truck chassis, and was armoured by Vickers. It could travel at about 25 mph on its wheels and 15 mph on its tracks. The vehicle proved unsatisfactory, being too complicated and unstable.

FWD RG7 (B4E3) mock-up, 1929. An early attempt at improving the cross-country performance of wheeled AFVs was this 6 × 6 rear-engined chassis, built by FWD Motors Ltd. It had a wooden mock-up hull but armour was never put on.

Vickers/Guy armoured car (Indian Pattern), 1929. One of the earliest British six-wheelers was the Guy 6 × 4 built for India. Note the supplementary tracks carried on the rear mudguards which could be applied to the rear wheels. It proved to be quite a good armoured car, albeit very heavy. It was first used by 10th Armoured Car Company RTC in 1928. The car weighed 9 tons and was powered by a 6-cylinder 120 bhp engine. In looks it was very similar to the Crossley but much larger.

Lanchester armoured car 6 × 4 experimental model A.
Known also as the Lanchester A, this experimental forerunner to the Mk I, had a single machine gun in the turret, which had a cupola across its width.

Lanchester armoured car 6 × 4 experimental model B.
Known also as the Lanchester B, this had a similar general look to the A, except that there were dual machine guns in the turret and the cupola was slightly different in shape.

Lanchester armoured car 6 × 4, Mark I, 1927. This was the first of a series of armoured cars to be produced by the Lanchester Motor Company, the first prototypes being ordered in 1927. It had a rigid chassis with drive to the rear wheels, which were double tyred. Its weight was about $7\frac{1}{2}$ tons. The armament comprised one Vickers .50 machine gun and one .303 in the turret, and another Vickers .303 in the hull alongside the driver. The crew was four men.

Crossley armoured car 30/70 hp, 1930. Three different Crossley six-wheeled chassis, the 30/70, 38/110, and 20/60 – all formed the basis of multi-wheeled armoured cars, one of the largest and earliest being the 30/70 hp medium chassis. The body was built by Vickers Armstrong and the car looked very much like the India Pattern Vickers Guy (see page 60), except for the very prominent radiator blower on the front. It weighed about 7.2 tons, had a crew of four and carried two Vickers machine guns. The cars were supplied to both the Army and RAF, as well as to other countries in the 1930s. Note the frame aerial array which was for ground to air communications.

Crossley armoured car 38/110 hp, 1930. Another car supplied to the RAF used an even more powerful engine, the 38/110 hp Crossley IGA4 series. Hull and turret were very like those of the Lanchester Mark 1, but there was only one machine gun in the turret.

Crossley light armoured car D2E1, 1928. Lightest of the six-wheeler chassis used was the 20/60 hp and there were two experimental models, the first being the D2E1. Ordered from the Royal Ordnance Factory in 1928, it had dual tyres at the rear and the turret from the Mark 1 light tank, and was armed with two Vickers machine guns, one in the turret, one in the hull. Note the tracks tied on to the rear mudguards which could be fixed to the rear wheels.

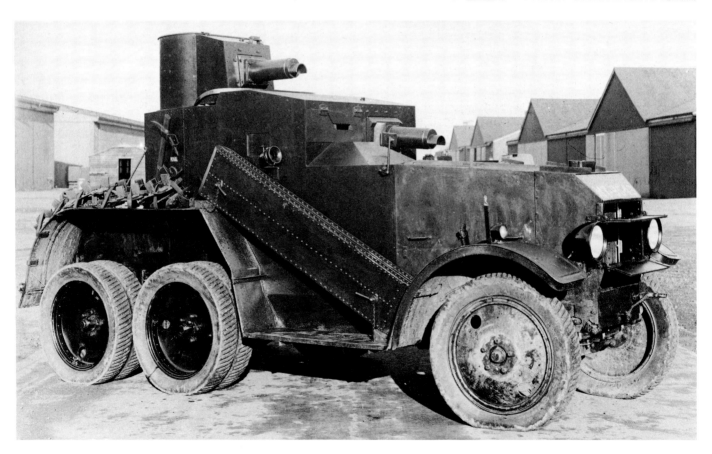

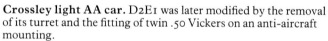

Crossley light AA car. D2E1 was later modified by the removal of its turret and the fitting of twin .50 Vickers on an anti-aircraft mounting.

Vickers Crossley light armoured car, 1928. The M28 model had single wheels all round, a three man crew, and one Vickers machine gun in the turret and one alongside the driver. Its 6-cylinder Crossley engine gave it a top speed of 40 mph.

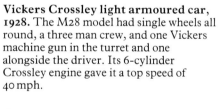

Crossley armoured car Mark 1. The production version of the experimental models had the contemporary light tank Mark 3 turret instead of that of the Mark 1. Two Crossley Mark 1s are seen at the head of this convoy.

Armstrong-Siddeley Pavesi. This was another experimental vehicle with an articulated hull. The driver and engine were in the front half and the load (a gun of some kind) in the rear. No armour was ever fitted and the vehicle did not go into production. A further experimental model was produced, slightly larger but still with no armour.

Armstrong-Siddeley armoured car 6 × 4. The general appearance of this armoured car was like the Alvis Straussler, with a low conical turret and a neat hull. It was built for the RAF but never went into production.

Scammel experimental armoured car. Not unlike the Lanchester Mk 1 at first glance, this 6 × 4 had a small additional turret on a platform at the rear. As the photograph shows, it was only completed as a part-wooden mock-up.

Vickers-Morris armoured car, 1931. Built specifically for Siam, this was based upon a Morris 2-ton commercial chassis with a small, round turret and double sets of tyres at the rear.

3 BETWEEN THE WARS
Austria

Berna-Perl armoured car, 1920 (*Top right*). After the Great War, Austria was not allowed to possess any armoured vehicles, except for a small number used by the police. One of these was this Berna-Perl, an Italian Lancia IZ hull and turret on a Perl chassis, with spoked wheels and solid tyres.

Schule Panzerauto, 1925 (*Right*). One of two training cars designed by Major Fritz Heigl who was a noted Austrian authority on armoured fighting vehicles. This earlier car had a cylindrical turret with a mounting for two machine guns. The second model, produced the following year, was very similar.

PA-2 Czech armoured car (*Below*). The Czechs built the PA-2 (nicknamed Zelva, or Turtle) in the early 1920s (see page 68), but Austria did not obtain its PA-2s until 1932. The Austrians added the small cupola in the centre.

ADGZ armoured car prototype, 1933 (*Right*). In 1933, the Austro-Daimler Company secretly began to design this large 8 × 8 armoured car, which was completed the following year. Weighing nearly $11\frac{3}{4}$ tons, it had a small eight-sided turret in the centre. Note that the centre wheels are closer together than the others.

ADGZ armoured car, 1935. In 1935, Austria renounced the peace treaty restrictions (as did Germany) and started producing AFVs openly. The ADGZ 1935 was not unlike the earlier 1933 model, but had a larger turret and carried machine guns front and rear in the hull, plus both heavy and light machine guns in the turret. It weighed 8 tons and was fitted with the Voith-Getriebe hydro-kinetic torque converter transmission.

ADGZ in Danzig, 1939. Here, an ADGZ armoured car is being used to support SS action against the Polish Post Office in Danzig, 1939.

ADKZ prototype armoured car. The second type of car produced by the Austro-Daimler Company was a 6 × 6, which had a much smaller hull and a low flat rear deck. The turret had large ball mounts for both heavy and light machine gun.

ADKZ armoured car, 1938. The production model of the ADKZ had rounded mudguards, a radio aerial around the turret and a very large ventilator between the two ball gun mountings. It was some $15\frac{1}{2}$ ft long, 7 ft 10 ins wide and nearly 8 ft high. Note the front rollers to help surmounting obstacles on cross country operations.

ADSK Kleinerpanzerwagen, 1937. This small silhouette 4 × 4 model had no turret and a very noticeable 'hump' at the rear over the engine.

ADSK Babyscout car. This model was very similar to the ADSK Kleinerpanzerwagen except that the glacis had a definite step in it. The vehicle had a machine gun alongside the driver. Note the driver's periscope (see also British section).

ADMK wheel-cum-track Mulus, 1935. This little wheel-cum-track carrier was designed to carry a single machine gun. There was also an unarmoured version used as a troop carrier.

Czechoslovakia

Ansaldo-Lancia (Italian) armoured car. The first two armoured cars in the Czechoslovak Army were Lancias which had been brought home after World War 1 by members of the Italian Legion. These cars were used in fighting against communist Hungary in 1919.

Fiat-Torino-Skoda, 1919. In 1919, Skoda, who owned the largest car manufacturing plant in Czechoslovakia, adapted 12 Fiat-Torino truck chassis as armoured cars. They were very tall and very heavy. Two Schwarzlose heavy machine guns were mounted in separate turrets, with all round traverse. They were still in service in 1929.

PA-1 armoured car, 1923. In 1922, the army placed an order with Skoda for the development of a new armoured car. The first two prototypes were completed the following year. The PA-1 had two machine guns, four-wheel drive and could be driven in either direction. The army did not like the car as it was too high and unstable. It weighed 6½ tons and had a crew of five. Its top speed was 32.5 mph.

PA-2 Zelva armoured car, 1925 (*Above left and above centre*). Because the army did not like the PA-1, Skoda took back the two prototypes and completely redesigned them, producing a really streamlined car with four machine guns in special ball mountings placed around the car to give all round fire. The resulting car was the

famous Zelva (Turtle), and the army ordered 12 of these 7.4-ton armoured cars; others were later sold to Austria (page 65). The Czech Army designation was OA vs 25. Zelva had a crew of five, a top speed of 70 km/h in either direction and a radius of action of 300 kms.

Skoda OA vs 29 armoured car, 1929. One Zelva was modified with the installation of a 75 mm gun, into the front plate, which increased its weight to 11 tons. It was so heavy and slow that it was never put into production.

PA-3 heavy armoured car, July 1927 (*Left and far left*). Known in the Czech Army as the OA vs 27, some 24 of these 6½-ton armoured cars were produced and remained in service until 1939. It was planned to improve the armament (all machine guns) by up-gunning with a 14.5 mm heavy machine gun or a 37 mm anti-tank gun, but this was not achieved. Note the searchlight mounted in the rear of the turret.

Skoda OA vs 27 armoured car. Close up of the turret of the OA vs 27, showing one of the Schwarzlose 7.92 mm vs machine guns.

Tatra 34 armoured car, 1929. Only one prototype of this light armoured car was produced by Tatra, but it was not accepted by the army, so never went into production.

Tatra 72 armoured car, 1930 (*Above and right*). Tatra were manufacturers of armoured cars in their factory in Moravia. Their second model, the Tatra 72, was accepted into service and designated OA vs 30. It was far more conventional in appearance than the Skoda cars, and was also light (3.6 tons) and had a good cross country performance. Some 50 were built for the army and, from 1939, 13 served with the Slovaks. With a crew of three, the car had a top speed of 37½ mph.

CKD (Praga) light armoured car, 1930 (*Below and below right*). CKD did not join in the development of military vehicles with Skoda and Tatra. They did, however, produce a light armoured car on their Praga truck chassis, which was used by the police.

3 BETWEEN THE WARS
China

Nationalist armoured car, 4 × 2. There were a number of improvised armoured cars like this one built on a Ford 3-ton chassis, originally used by the Shanghai Volunteer Force, and then inherited by the Nationalist Forces.

Nationalist armoured car 6 × 4, 1933 (*Below*). This version had a conventional hull and a single low octagonal turret, with several machine guns in ball mountings. It would appear to have been built on a standard British 30 cwt chassis and was possibly constructed in either Singapore or Hong Kong.

Nationalist armoured car 6 × 4, 1933 (*Above*). Otherwise very similar to the model in the previous photograph, this car had two diagonally placed turrets with bevelled sides. These cars were actually photographed during 1942, in the Canton area, when they were being used for training.

Semi-armoured motorcycle. Behind another 6 × 4 with dual turrets in this march past is a semi-armoured motor-cycle, a type obtained from the Germans in the 1930s. Note the armoured shield for the driver and the machine gun mounted in the sidecar.

German light armoured car Sd Kfz 222. First built in 1936, this Leichter Panzerspahwagen was armed with one 20 mm KwK30 and one MG34. They are seen here in service with the Chinese army in a review in Yunnan Province during the war.

American M3 scout car. Many thousands of armoured vehicles, including these M3 scout cars, were sent by the USA to such countries as China and Russia during World War 2. They are seen here during a military review for Lung Yun, Governor of Yunnan Province. The M3 scout cars are preceded in the parade by German SD Kfz 222s.

Russian BA-6 and BA-27 armoured cars. Other foreign armoured cars in Chinese service during World War 2 were these Russian armoured cars, the BA-6, nearest the camera, and BA-27 four-wheelers.

Eire

Improvised armoured car, 1916. Strictly speaking, this improvised car should be in the World War 1 section because it was built in 1916 and was used during the Easter rising in that year, when the Sinn Feiners rose in Dublin and were subsequently suppressed and their leaders executed. The car was based upon a Daimler chassis, one of the Guinness Breweries fleet, which was armoured by the Inchicore Railway workshop, near Dublin.

Lancia armoured car, 1922 (*Below right and far right*). After Irish independence in the early 1920s, various types of armoured cars were used, such as Rolls-Royce, Peerless and these Lancias. The sides were increased in height and loopholes provided for use by those inside. A V-shaped mesh roof was added to keep out missiles. They were nicknamed 'Hooded Terrors'. Some had flanged wheels fitted and were used for patrolling on railways. One such car had a cylindrical turret and box-like hull.

Landsverk L-180 armoured car, 1936 (*Left*). The Irish Armoured Car Corps was formally constituted in August 1922 and was equipped with Rolls-Royce, Peerless and Lancia cars – some 84 armoured cars in all. It was not until the early 1930s that any new vehicles were purchased, some of the best being from the Landsverk Company of Sweden (see later). Initially, two cars (ZC 757, seen here, and ZC 758) were purchased, followed later by six more. Weighing 7½ tons, they mounted a Madsen 20 mm cannon and coaxial machine gun, with a second machine gun beside the driver. Duplicate driving controls were fitted at the rear.

Landsverk L-180 armoured car. This photograph shows the front view of one of the additional six L-180 cars mentioned above. They were delivered in 1936. Two years later, it was proposed to purchase a further 14, but, for financial reasons, this was cut to six and was so delayed that the outbreak of World War 2 prevented their delivery. Nearly all the cars were still serving in the early 1980s.

Leyland armoured car, 1938 (*Right and below*). In 1934, a Leyland Terrier chassis was purchased for the purpose of modernising one of the Peerless cars (twin-turreted), but, after trials, it was decided to replace the twin turrets with a single large one. To standardise with the Landsverk L60 tanks which were then arriving, it was decided to model the turret on the Landsverk's and, later, to actually purchase four Landsverk turrets. Construction of the first car began in 1937, and four cars (Nos ZC 773–ZC 776) were subsequently taken into service with 1st Armoured Squadron in July 1939. After World War 2, they were re-engined. All except ZC 775 were still in service in 1980.

3 BETWEEN THE WARS

France

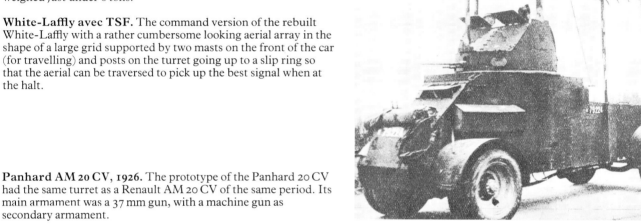

White-Laffly, automitrailleuse, 1925. During the Great War, several hundred White-Laffly were built (see Part 2, Section 5). Over 200 continued in service after the Armistice. In the 1920s, those remaining were rebuilt with a raised hull, pneumatic tyres and other modern features. The car's crew was four and it weighed just under 6 tons.

White-Laffly avec TSF. The command version of the rebuilt White-Laffly with a rather cumbersome looking aerial array in the shape of a large grid supported by two masts on the front of the car (for travelling) and posts on the turret going up to a slip ring so that the aerial can be traversed to pick up the best signal when at the halt.

Panhard AM 20 CV, 1926. The prototype of the Panhard 20 CV had the same turret as a Renault AM 20 CV of the same period. Its main armament was a 37 mm gun, with a machine gun as secondary armament.

Panhard AMD 165/175 TOE, 1933. This later model of the AM 20 CV, renamed as the AMD Panhard 165/175 TOE, had a remodelled turret and larger wheels. Weighing 6.7 tons, it had 9 mm armour, a top speed of 75 km/h and a range of 750 km.

Panhard AMD 178, 1934 (*Above left*). The prototype of this automitrailleuse de decouverte (distant recce) was built in 1933. The first production models were produced the following year. It was the main successor to the White-Laffly. It was armed with a 25 mm cannon. Its armour was of 13 mm maximum thickness, and weighed 8.2 tons. The 8-cylinder Panhard engine gave it a top speed of 72 km/h, while it had a range of 300 km.

Panhard AMD 178 command version (*Above*). On the command version of the Panhard AMD 178, the armament was removed, but the mounting remained. The large aerial would be for the powerful radio set which occupied most of the turret.

Berliet 4 × 4 VUDB, 1929. The Lyonnaise firm of Berliet built various armoured cars between the wars, one of the earliest being this 'Voiture de prise de contact' (literally: vehicle to make contact) which had a crew of three men and weighed 4.95 tons, and was first built in prototype form in 1929. Berliet received an order to build 50 for the French army the following year and later a further 12 were built for the Belgians. The cars saw service with the French army in North Africa. It had a top speed of 53 km/h.

Berliet Type VUM, 1930. Also known as the automitrailleuse 'Syrie', this conventional armoured car was produced in prototype form in 1930 by Berliet and was built for service with the French army in Syria. No further cars of this type were built. Weighing 7.6 tons, it had a crew of four and mounted two machine guns in the turret. It was 4.3 m long, 2.12 m wide and 1.68 m high.

Berliet AMR VUD B4, 1932. This automitrailleuse de reconnaissance (AMR) was built and tested in 1932. It weighed 4.95 tons and had a top speed of 53 km/h. Four models were ordered by the French army. However, after trials, it was decided that it was too heavy, too visible and insufficiently armed (just one machine gun), although its cross country performance was satisfactory.

Berliet AMD VUB, 1931/32. Presented to the Commission de Vincennes in 1933, this automitrailleuse de decouverte (AMD) was built by Berliet and weighed 7.75 tons. The photograph shows it from the rear. It had a top speed of 72 km/h. Armament was one 25 mm Hotchkiss cannon.

Gendron AMR Somua, 1934 (*Below and below right*). Also known as the AMR Gendron Poniatowski, this AMR had a box-like hull, curved at the rear with side louvres (lettered A and B on the original of the right photograph) and moveable metal wheels in the centre to be used on cross country driving. The turret, which was from a Renault VM tank, was centrally located.

Gendron AMR Somua, 1935 (*Above and above right*). The next prototype was very similar to the 1934 model, but, this time, the centre wheels were pneumatic and fitted with cleated tyre chains.

Gendron AMR Somua, 1935 modified. The next modification to the Gendron Somua was the installation of a cylindrical turret in which it was intended to mount a 25 mm cannon and a machine gun.

Gendron AMR Somua 39. The final Gendron Somua prototype emerged in 1938 and was followed the next year by this production model. Now weighing 6.5 tons, it had a much better performance, and mounted a 25 mm anti-tank gun and a 7.5 mm machine gun in a well-shaped turret. It had a top speed of 69 km/h and a radius of action of 400 kms and its dimensions were 3.745 m × 2.05 m × 1.60 m.

Laffly AMD 80 AM (series). Laffly began work on this series of armoured cars, also called the 'Laffly Vincennes', in 1931, producing various prototypes until the armoured car was finally accepted in late 1934 and put into production. They went on to serve in North Africa and were still in use against the Germans and Italians in late 1942. Weighing 7.5 tons, the 80 AM had a top speed of 80 km/h and a range of 400 km. It was armed with a 13.2 mm machine gun, and had a crew of four. Its dimensions were: 5.7 m long, 2.1 m high and 1.8 m wide. After the war they were used in Algeria, 1945–46.

Renault AMD, 1931/32 (*Below*). Another armoured car which did not reach production was the Renault AMD. It weighed just over 6 tons, had a top speed of 75.78 km/h and a crew of three, and mounted a 20 mm cannon and a 7.5 mm machine gun. Various modifications were made to improve its performance, but the basic problem was lack of space in the small turret and trials were terminated in March 1934. It was not adopted by the French army.

Saurer, 1930 (*Above*). Used in Morocco and Algeria for convoy protection by the Compagnie Africaine de Transports, this armoured car with its distinctive octagonal turret, had plenty of room in the hull and good ventilation as it had to be used in desert conditions. Its dimensions were: 5.96 m long, 1.98 m wide, and 2.61 m high.

Berliet Type VPDM, 1931. Another armoured car to be specially constructed for use by the French army in Morocco was this multi-wheel 8-ton AFV (ten wheels, the back eight being driven). It had a top speed of 66 km/h. Only one prototype was constructed, in 1931, and it was not put into production.

Berliet Type UDB4, 1934. Produced in 1934/35, this 6 × 6 armoured car had both front and rear driving positions and a small turret centrally placed on top.

Laffly S 14 TOE prototype, 1934 (*Below*). In 1934, Laffly at Fontainbleau produced an experimental vehicle which resembled a troop transport. However, it was the prototype for their AMD, and comprised the chassis S 15 with an armoured body on top (no turret at this stage). The small wheels at the front were to help the vehicle to get out of obstacles.

Laffly S 15 TOE series vehicle (*Above*). The Laffly car which actually came into service had a small hemispherical turret on top of the body and was used both as an armoured car and an armoured personnel carrier (APC). At least 25 were built for the French army. The 15 TOE weighed 5 tons, had a top speed of 60 km/h and a range of 1,000 km. Its normal crew was three, but it could carry eight men as an APC.

Laffly S 15 TOE command version. The two Laffly nearest the camera have mountings for large aerial bases (only one has the antenna fitted) on the front mudguard, plus a second aerial base block on top of the small turret.

Laffly S 15 with SP gun. This version of the Laffly S 15, had an armoured body, lower than the TOE and with a 47 mm field gun with shield, mounted on the rear so that it became an SP gun.

EBR, 1937. The 1937 model was very similar to the post-World War 2 EBR, a twin-gun AA version of which is illustrated here. It had a large centre-mounted turret, low hull and a centre pair of wheels that could be lowered for cross country work. It was never put into production.

Panhard AMR, 1938. Also known as the AMD 201, this model was built and completed by December 1939. It had a crew of three, an oscillating turret containing a 25 mm gun and a 7.5 mm coaxial machine gun. When World War 2 broke out, the AFV was taken across to North Africa, in 1940, in order to avoid capture by the Germans. It was subsequently buried to escape detection when the German disarmament commission visited there. It has never been found.

Schneider Laurent amphibious wheel-cum-track, 1930 (*Below left*). Little is known about this strange looking AFV, which had wheels (only the rear axle carried double wheels) and, behind them, tracks. Also, on the rear of the vehicle it is just possible to make out some type of water propulsion. It did not get further than prototype stage.

Schneider AMC P16 (M 29) series vehicle (*Below*). Just one example of the numerous half-track vehicles that were used for reconnaissance and other armoured car work between the mid-1920s and World War 2. Weighing 6.8 tons, it was armed with a 37 mm cannon and a 7.5 mm machine gun. The half-track had a top speed of 50 km/h and a range of 250 km.

3 BETWEEN THE WARS
Germany

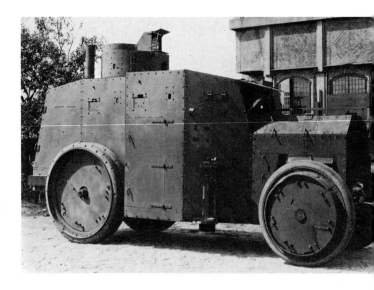

Daimler Gepanzerten Kraftwagen, Sd Kfz 3, 1919. This vehicle was built on a wartime four-wheel drive tractor chassis, with rear wheels of larger diameter than the front wheels. Police armoured personnel carriers of this type were permitted under the terms of the Treaty of Versailles and were never intended for military use. This model had a crew of six and armour up to 10 mm thick, and was powered by a Daimler 100 hp petrol engine. About 30 were built at Daimler's Stuttgart works. It had a top speed of 50 km/h and a range of 300 km.

Daimler DZVR, 1919. The DZVR was the same as the Sd Kfz 3, but did not have the turret. Despite having four wheel drive, the cars were road-bound and quite unsuitable for cross country work. Also known as the Schuposonderwagen.

Daimler DZVR, Schuposonderwagen, 1921. This model was later also known as the Sd Kfz 3. Unlike the 1919 version, it had wheels of the same diameter, this turretless version was used as an APC by the Reichswehr.

Benz VP21 Schuposonderwagen, 1921.
The three police vehicles nearest the camera are VP21s, which had two rotating machine gun turrets and an observation tower in between. They were later taken over for use by the army. The armoured body was made by Martini & Huneke of Salzkotten. The last car in the row is a 1919 Daimler.

Bussing Strassenpanzerwagen, 1928 (*Below*). This was the first simulated armoured car to be built after Germany had decided to re-arm. It was not unlike the Czech Zelva but had a large, wide cylindrical turret. It did not have rear steering and was built upon a Bussing commercial lorry chassis, in Hannover, in 1928.

Benz VP21, 1921. German police pose round their Schuposonderwagen.

Adler training car, 1929. Also known as the Adler Standard 6, this simulated armoured car was used for recce training. It had a conventional appearance apart from the stroboscope on the top of the turret.

BMW Dixi Type 3/15, 1929 (*Above and above right*). The Dixi was a licence-built version of the British Austin 7 on to which was bolted simulated armour to make a 'tank' for training purposes. Both the armour and armament were made out of wood and canvas.

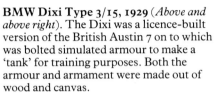

Mannschaftstransportwagen 1, Daimler-Benz prototype, 1928. In 1927, orders were placed with various firms to produce experimental recce vehicles. Each firm produced two prototype vehicles, all weighing about $7\frac{1}{2}$ tons. One was this eight-wheeler from Daimler-Benz, which was powered by a 6-cylinder 1000PS engine. The crew was to be five men. Magirus developed a similar vehicle powered by the same engine. Both were designed to swim. The vehicle is seen here during cross country trials.

Mannschaftstransportwagen 1, Magirus prototype, 1928. Rheinmetall Borsig developed a turret for the experimental recce vehicle requested in 1927 which was to mount a 37 mm gun and a 7.92 mm machine gun, seen here on one of the Magirus prototypes. It carried 66 rounds of ammunition for the 37 mm.

Mannschaftstransportwagen 1, Bussing-NAG prototype, 1929. The third firm asked in 1927 to produce prototypes, Bussing-NAG, in contrast to Daimler-Benz and Magirus, produced a larger 10 × 10 wheeled vehicle which was also known as the Schwimmwagen ZRW. It had cork-filled boxes over the wheels to assist flotation. It was tested extensively in Germany and Russia.

Mannschaftstransportwagen 1, cork-bodied prototype. One of the eight-wheel versions had this cork-filled body built on to it in place of the more streamlined metal one, for swimming trials. In early 1930, it was decided that the Mannschaftstransportwagen was going to be too expensive to produce, so the project was dropped. However, much of the research work was later used in designing the eight-wheeled Sd Kfz 231 (see page 152).

Maschinengewehrkraftwagen Adler Kfz 13, 1932 (*Left*). The first of the new recce vehicles for the expanding German army was this small, 2.1 ton, four-wheeler built by Adlerwerke, with 8 mm armour attached to a standard 4 × 4 passenger car chassis. The armament was provided by a pedestal mounted MG 13. The crew of this light recce car was two and it had a top speed of 70 km/h and a range of 300 km. About 150 were built between 1932 and 1934. They saw service in both Poland and France, but were withdrawn from service during 1941.

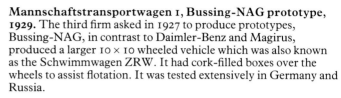

Funkkraftwagen Adler Kfz 14, 1932 (*Right*). Supporting the Kfz 13 was this radio car, the Kfz 14 (seen second in this photograph). When used in this role, the vehicle was fitted with a long range frame aerial to provide mobile communications, the crew was three and the pedestal-mounted machine gun was removed. Approximately 40 Kfz 14 were produced.

Krupp gepanzerter Radfahrzeug, 1936. Based upon the standard chassis of the Krupp L2H 143 1½-ton 6 × 4 lorry, this 5.2-ton armoured car was produced from 1936 and a number were sold to the Netherlands for use in the Dutch East Indies. It had a five-man crew, and the original version, seen here, had a single machine gun in a small turret. The production model had two machine guns front and rear in the hull as well as one turret-mounted machine gun.

Krupp gepanzerter Radfahrzeug, 1936 (*Above right and right*). These photographs were taken in the yard of the ruined Reichstag building in Berlin in 1945 and show one of the production models of the Krupp armoured car, somewhat battered! In front of it are the remains of an equally battered Benz VP21 Schuposonderwagen (already described on page 83); in the top right photograph, a British officer is standing beside the VP21.

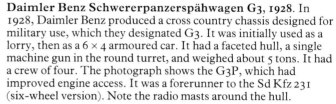

Daimler Benz Schwererpanzerspähwagen G3, 1928. In 1928, Daimler Benz produced a cross country chassis designed for military use, which they designated G3. It was initially used as a lorry, then as a 6 × 4 armoured car. It had a faceted hull, a single machine gun in the round turret, and weighed about 5 tons. It had a crew of four. The photograph shows the G3P, which had improved engine access. It was a forerunner to the Sd Kfz 231 (six-wheel version). Note the radio masts around the hull.

PzSpWg G3aP, 1932. This later version had a slightly shorter wheelbase and a more sloping radiator, while the glacis was stepped to incorporate a driver's vision slot. It first appeared on manoeuvres in 1932.

PzSpWg G3a prototype. Close-up of one of the early prototype models of the G3a, showing the rear steering wheel and driver's cowl. The round, rear hull door is open, while the original six-sided turret with large crew access hatches is visible – compare this with the rounded turret on the later models.

3 BETWEEN THE WARS
Hungary

Csaba 39 Mpcgk, 1939. After the various Straussler designs (which have already been covered in Part 3, Section 1, Great Britain), came the only Hungarian armoured car to be designed by Straussler for 'home consumption'. Produced before Hungary came under German control in 1939, it had a 20 mm gun and a machine gun in the neatly shaped turret. It was a three-man vehicle with the turret crew of two sitting directly behind the driver. It was 14 ft 9 ins long, 6 ft 10 ins wide, and 7 ft 5 ins high. Although they remained in service until 1942, the small number of Csaba 39s built never saw active service, but may have been used for IS duties.

3 BETWEEN THE WARS
Italy

Ansaldo big wheel armoured car, 1929. This odd looking three-man, 4.6 m long armoured car weighed about 8.25 tons, and had four articulated, solid-spoked wheels with large grousers, and steered on the rear axle only. There were two versions, one mounting a 37 mm and the other a long barrelled 47 mm, plus a machine gun. Note the concentric radiator louvres.

Bianchi autoblindata, 1931. This was a modernised version of Bianchi's World War 1 car (not illustrated), with the old Bianchi hull mounted on a Spa 38r truck chassis, and an open-top low turret and pneumatic tyres. The armour was no more than ¼ in thick and a single machine gun was carried. They were designed for use in Tripoli.

Carro AA Ceirano 50 CMA 175CK, 1928. This vehicle consisted of a 5-ton lorry with a pedestal mounted 75 mm AA gun. The lorry had drop sides and was 20 ft long.

Corni-Scognamiglio (Nebiolo), 1930. This light armoured car had a rounded, moulded hull with a ball-mounted machine gun on the left of the driver and an AA machine gun pedestal mounted inside the hull. It was only partially armoured. The doors in the sides give it almost the appearance of a passenger car.

Pavesi big wheel armoured car P4, 1924. Also known as the 30PS, this two-man 4.2-ton big-wheeled car had the turret of a Renault FT light tank, mounting a single machine gun. Its top speed was 17 km/h. It was steered (as with all those built on the Pavesi principle) by chassis articulation and was driven on all wheels.

Pavesi 2, 1925. The next Pavesi model (also known as the 35 PS) weighed 5 tons and had a larger turret and hull than its predecessor but was otherwise very similar. It had a top speed of 30 km/h.

Pavesi L 140 heavy model, 1925. This car had a machine gun in the front plate, another in the turret and a third in the rear. Its crew was four. It weighed 5.5 tons.

Pavesi Ante Carro, 1925. The anti-tank version of the Pavesi was a three-man, $5\frac{1}{2}$-ton car, with a 57 mm gun mounted in the front plate and a small forward cupola in place of a turret.

Fiat 611 multi-wheeled armoured car, 1934. From the early 1930s, Fiat Ansaldo began work on a new, large, multi-wheel armoured car with a crew of five. The first model, in 1932, was armed only with machine guns. The 611B, however, had a 47 mm gun in the seven-sided turret as its main armament. Weighing just under 7 tons, the 6×4 car was over 15 ft long and had a top speed of 47 mph forward and 25 mph in reverse – it could be driven in either direction.

Japan

Vickers Crossley Type 87, 1927. Amongst the earliest armoured cars in Japanese service was the British 1925 Indian pattern Vickers Crossley armoured car, which they bought in 1927 and later modified by fitting pneumatic tyres (see car in the photograph *right*). One photograph shows two Vickers Crossleys supporting Japanese sailors in a sandbagged emplacement in China during the war there; the Japanese flag on the side denotes that it is a naval car.

Sumida Type ARM, 1928. This very conventional looking armoured car was produced in the same year as the Japanese motor car industry was officially started. Based upon an Osaka chassis with heavy spoked wheels and solid tyres, its box hull carried a conical turret containing one ball-mounted machine gun. Osaka was the location of the Japanese Artillery Arsenal.

Osaka Type 2592, 1932. Not unlike the Sumida ARM, this four- or five-man, 6-ton 8-cwt armoured car had two machine guns, the one in the turret being on a sliding traverse mount which operated through the large elongated slot. To understand the Japanese system of numbering their cars, one must first understand their calendar. This started with the legendary founding of the Japanese Empire in 660 BC, so to equate with our calendar one must subtract 660 from the year. They used the year to denote vehicle type number, thus, the Type 2592 was built in AD 1932 (i.e. 2592 minus 660). After the Japanese year 2601 (AD 1941), they used only the last digit to denote the type number.

Dowa, 1939 (*Left and far left*). This was possibly a local modification to the British Crossley, in which the dome turret was removed and a stationary turret substituted, mounting two air-cooled machine guns. Note the tall commander's cupola. The running boards were detachable for use when crossing ditches. The name Dowa is suspect.

Bedford, 1933. Several of these armoured personnel carriers were built. They had an anti-grenade fence around the top of the long box hull.

Naval pattern M2592, 1932 (*Below and right*). This naval pattern 6 × 4 armoured car weighed 6.2 tons, had a crew of six, a top speed of 80 km/h and armour between 8 and 11 mm thick. It was 4.8 m long, 1.8 m wide, and 2.3 m tall. It mounted a total of five machine guns.

Chigoda TGE 2590, 1930. Major Fritz Heigl, the famous Austrian authority on tanks and armoured cars, calls this car the Sumida M2590, and it is certainly similar to the M2593 (next photograph), but the turret had a flat top. It would appear that this car was also adaptable for railway use. (Heigl's series of books, published between the wars, *Taschenbuch der Tanks*, were, and still are, the source of much information on AFV's of all nations up to 1938.

Sumida M2953, 1933. In addition to the domed turret, this car has a smaller observation hatch in the roof, presumably for use by passengers in the large body. The M2593 had a crew of six, a top speed of 60 km/h and armour up to 16 mm thick. It was adaptable for use on the railways, the flanged rims being carried on the sides of the car.

Sumida M2953, railway use (*Below*). This photograph of the Sumida M2953 shows it adapted for rail use – the road tyres are now on both sides of the car. It also gives an excellent view of the jack/roller unit which was mounted back and front for use in conjunction with the short lengths of rail also carried on the hull, for getting the car on and off the railway. It was 6.57 m long, 1.9 m wide, and 2.95 m high.

Inoma-Kaminishi wheel-cum-track, 1928. This was the first of a series of experimental wheel-cum-track amphibians, with Kegresse type suspension. The drive and steering and the power take-off for a propellor unit were on the rear axle. It could travel equally fast in either direction.

Ishikawajime amphibious half track, 1930. These two photographs show the AFV with and without a turret. It had a crew of two, weighed 2.5 tons and had armour 5 mm thick. Its top speed on land was 45 km/h and in the water 9 km/h. It was not adopted for service.

3 BETWEEN THE WARS
Netherlands

Ehrhardt-Siderus, 1919. Some German M1917 Ehrhardt cars were rebuilt by the Dutch Siderus company after World War 1 for use by the Dutch police. Note the different turret on this 8.3-ton, three- or four-man car, which carried a single machine gun and had armour varying between 6 and 12 mm thick.

Bison, 1925 (*Above*). Improvised armoured car with an armoured box-like hull, built on to a 4 × 2 lorry chassis. Note the disc wheels with solid tyres. It mounted one machine gun in the dome-shaped turret and two (one just visible over the officer's shoulder) in the rear hull.

Police armoured car (*Above right*). Also used for police work, probably as an APC, this vehicle had a top speed of 45 km/h and could carry seven men.

M38 Swedish Landsverk. In the 1930s, the Dutch purchased some Swedish Landsverk armoured cars, both the L180 which they called M36 and the L182 (pictured here) which was known as the M38. (See Section 16 for the descriptions of these cars.)

DAF M39 Panserwagen, 1938 (*Top, centre and bottom left*). This was the production model of the Van Dorne Type 3, 6 × 4, armoured car which had appeared in prototype form in 1937. It had large engine louvres on the top of the hull at the rear, a 20 mm gun and coaxial machine gun in the turret and two machine guns in the hull, front and rear. Two small wheels were added at the front of the hull to prevent bellying. The dimensions of this 6-ton car were 4.63 m long, 2 m high and 2 m wide. Taken over by the Germans when Holland was occupied, the Van Dorne armoured cars were used for IS duties and known as the PzSpWg DAF 201 (h), as the *bottom left* photograph shows.

Krupp armoured personnel carrier, 1936. These German-built APCs were used in the Dutch East Indies.

Improvised armoured car. One of a number of improvised armoured cars used in the Dutch East Indies, probably based on a Ford chassis. Others were based on Chrysler, GMC and Van Dorne civilian-built vehicles.

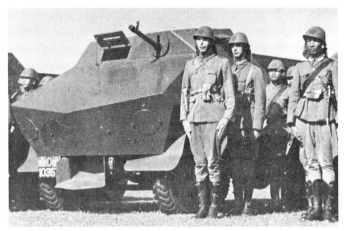

Braat armoured personnel carriers. Two versions of Braat armoured vehicles used in the Dutch East Indies and Batavia are seen here, an APC (*left*), and one (*below left*) only used in an AA role.

AA lorry. Seen here on maneouvres in Java is a column of truck-mounted AA heavy machine guns. Chassis used for this purpose were again of many different makes.

3 BETWEEN THE WARS
Norway

Improvised training car, 1935. Norway produced a number of simulated armoured cars for training purposes during the mid-1930s, such as these two based on a Chevrolet 4 × 2 chassis. The crew was apparently two and the armament a single machine gun in the turret. Norway later purchased a few Swedish L185 armoured cars. (This is probably the only photograph of a Norwegian armoured car of the period in existence.)

3 BETWEEN THE WARS
Poland

Ford type Tfc, 1919. The Poles made use of various armoured cars during the Russo-Polish war which followed the recreation of Poland after World War 1. In addition to captured armoured cars, they improvised others, using, for example, the model T Ford chassis. Tyres were pneumatic and filled with glycerine for self-sealing. A single Maxim machine gun was mounted in the turret of this very cramped little armoured car.

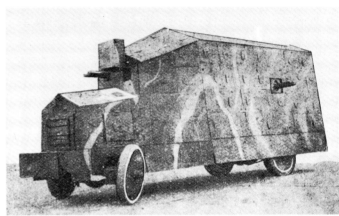

Bukowski armoured personnel carrier, 1926. Based on a Packard chassis, this armoured personnel carrier was developed in the mid-1920s but was not put into full production. It had segmented armour which was covered in rifle portholes. It mounted machine guns front, rear and sides.

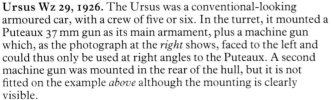

Ursus Wz 29, 1926. The Ursus was a conventional-looking armoured car, with a crew of five or six. In the turret, it mounted a Puteaux 37 mm gun as its main armament, plus a machine gun which, as the photograph at the *right* shows, faced to the left and could thus only be used at right angles to the Puteaux. A second machine gun was mounted in the rear of the hull, but it is not fitted on the example *above* although the mounting is clearly visible.

Ursus Wz 34 I and II. Another version of the Ursus had a somewhat stubbier hull than the Wz 29 and a turret with a cupola on top, exactly like the hull and turret on the Polish version of the Citroën-Kegresse half-track bought from France at about the same time. As the photograph at the *right* shows, there were two versions, one with a machine gun in the turret, and the other with the 37 mm cannon. The Ursus armoured cars remained in service up to the German invasion but proved ineffective against the more sophisticated AFVs of their opponents.

Russia

BA-27, 1927. The first armoured cars to be developed in the USSR after World War I did not appear until after the start of the First Five-Year Plan in 1927, when production of AFVs began on a large scale. For example, it was envisaged that the mechanised brigades of the Red Army would each have a force of 56 armoured cars, while there would be 215 per mechanised corps. This first car, the BA-27, was based on the GAZ-A Ford four-seater car. Although normally known by the initials BA, standing for *Bronieavtomobil* (armoured automobile), the A was sometimes dropped. Weighing $4\frac{1}{2}$ tons, the BA-27 had rivetted armour varying in thickness between 6 and 13 mm. Its crew was two to four men, and its armament comprised a 37 mm tank gun and a 7.62 coaxial machine gun, both in separate ball mountings. It was 14.82 ft long, 5.93 ft wide, and 8 ft high. The car had a top speed of 28 mph and a range of 80 miles.

FA-1, 1930 (*Above and above left*). Like the BA-27, this car was based on a GAZ Model A chassis but now had angled side armour and spoked rather than solid wheels. Weighing 3.2 tons, the new car mounted either one or two machine guns in a small, domed turret. The crew of two were very cramped. It was 12.15 ft long, 5.41 ft wide and 6.32 ft high. Its top speed was 50 mph and its radius of action 125 miles. Armour was 8–9 mm thick.

FA-2, 1930. A second version was produced, this time without a turret. Known also as the Bronieford (armoured saloon), it had an open top with a pedestal-mounted 7.62 mm DT tank machine gun. It weighed only 2.1 tons. Its armour was 5–6 mm thick. Drive like the FA-1, was only to the rear axle of this 9.88 ft × 4.27 ft × 8.66 ft car.

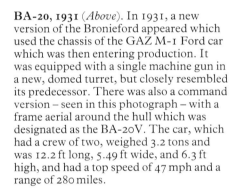

BA-20, 1931 (*Above*). In 1931, a new version of the Bronieford appeared which used the chassis of the GAZ M-1 Ford car which was then entering production. It was equipped with a single machine gun in a new, domed turret, but closely resembled its predecessor. There was also a command version – seen in this photograph – with a frame aerial around the hull which was designated as the BA-20V. The car, which had a crew of two, weighed 3.2 tons and was 12.2 ft long, 5.49 ft wide, and 6.3 ft high, and had a top speed of 47 mph and a range of 280 miles.

BA-20 Sh.d. This version of the BA-20 was specially adapted for railway use, and had the additional designation Sh.d (*Shelesnaya Doroga*, which means railway).

BA-20M. A new model of the BA-20 was produced later which was of welded construction throughout and had a whip-type aerial on the left-hand side of the hull in place of the frame type. It weighed only $2\frac{1}{2}$ tons, and had a top speed of 55 mph and a range of 280 miles. It was 14.11 ft long, 5.74 ft wide and 7 ft high.

BA-20M Sh.d (*Above right*). As with the BA-20 model, the BA-20M could be adapted for use as a railcar. This one was taken over by the Germans during World War 2.

BA-6T medium armoured car (*Right*). This car also appeared during the First Five-Year Plan and had a square-cut, welded turret taken from the T-26B light tank which mounted either a 37 mm or 45 mm long tank gun. Weighing 7 tons, it was of similar size and performance to the BA-3. The BA-6 saw service during the Spanish Civil War, which is where this example was photographed.

BA-3 medium armoured car. Also produced in the First Five-Year Plan was a medium multi-wheel armoured car, the BA-3. The original model had rivetted armour, but later welded armour was used. The 5.2-ton car had a small turret like that on the BA-20, mounting either a 37 mm or 12.7 mm heavy machine gun. With a top speed of 35 mph and a range of 160 miles, this four-man car was 15.3 ft long, 6.9 ft wide, and 7.2 ft high. A single row of BA-3s are seen here behind some BA-20s.

BAZ Amfibyi (*Left and far left*). There was also an amphibibus version of the BA-6, designated BAZ (or BAD), which had a distinctive boat-shaped hull. The chassis was that of a Ford AAA three-axled lorry. The turret was fully rotating and mounted a 37 mm gun. There were two front sponsons in addition to the turret, the right one for a machine gun, while the left was for the driver. There was also an auxiliary turret at the rear behind the main turret, with another machine gun with limited traverse (270 degrees). The dimensions of this four-man car were: 21.3 ft in length, 6.9 ft in width, and 7.2 ft in height.

BA-10 armoured car, 1934 (*Above, left and centre left and right*). All the BA-10's main features are covered in the all-round views given by these four photographs. Sometimes known as the BA-32, this multi-wheel medium armoured car had the same hull as earlier six-wheel types but mounted the turret of the T-30 light tank, which had a 45 mm semi-automatic tank gun. The secondary armament comprised one 7.62 mm machine gun in the turret and one next to the driver. The car's weight was 5.2 tons and it had armour 10 mm thick. Its top speed was 35 mph and its range 185 miles. The later BA-10M model, which appeared in 1937, had a pressed and welded hull and weighed slightly more. All models had tracks which could be fitted around the rear wheels to improve cross-country performance.

Spain

Heavy armoured car M28, 1921 (*Right and below right*). Weighing 8-tons, this eight-man armoured car carried either four machine guns or one 3.7 cm gun and one machine gun. It was capable of a speed of 45 km/h forwards and 40 km/h in reverse. The armour was up to 12 mm thick. This primitive car was in government service before the Civil War.

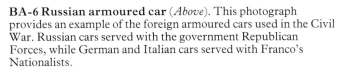

BA-6 Russian armoured car (*Above*). This photograph provides an example of the foreign armoured cars used in the Civil War. Russian cars served with the government Republican Forces, while German and Italian cars served with Franco's Nationalists.

Carro Blindado Bilbao, 1936 (*Right, below and below right*). Two very similar cars are illustrated here, both of which use Dodge chassis, but one has an octagonal, the other a cylindrical turret. They were used by the government police.

Camion Blindado, Republican, 1935.
The basis for this Republican car was a
1935 Chevrolet. It weighed 2,655 kg, and
was 5.56 m long, 1.98 m wide, and 2.99 m
high. It could carry up to 15 men
(commander, driver and 13 riflemen). It
was possible to fire rifles through the side
ports and the triangular openings front and
rear. The armour plate was up to 6 mm
thick. Franco began the civil war by
invading Spain from Morocco in 1936.

Camion Blindado 'Durruti'. Two
women members of the Government
Forces walk past a captured armoured car
en route to the battle area of the Aragon
Front, 30 September 1936. The car had
belonged to La Columna Durruti of the
Nationalist Forces, but now carries a
Republican flag.

Camion Blindado, Republican, 1936.
This car was photographed in Madrid in
November 1936. Eight riflemen, four each
side, could fire through the rifle ports.
Franco's Nationalists initially failed to take
Madrid, meeting determined resistance
organised by the trade unions.

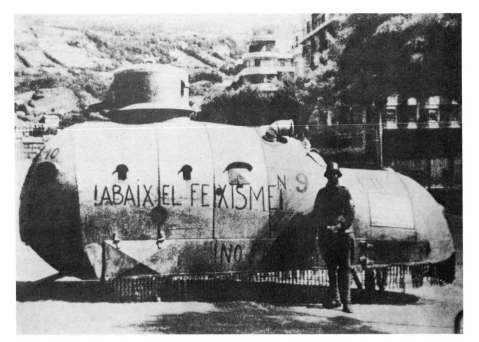

Camion Blindado Barcelona. Another Government car was this grotesque looking monster from the Constructora Field of Barcelona. It weighed about 3,400 kg and could carry either eight or nine men (commander, driver and up to seven riflemen). Note the odd 'chain-mail' skirt, presumably to protect the wheels.

Nationalist armoured cars (*Below and below left*). Two of the makeshift armoured cars constructed by the insurgents are seen here in Valencia in 1936. After the bitterly fought Battle of the Ebro (July–November 1938), the Loyalist Forces were exhausted. Nationalist troops entered Madrid at the end of March 1939 and the war officially ended on 1 April.

Camion Blindado Renault ADR, 1937 (*Left*). Based on the Renault, this trio of large Republican improvised armoured cars had a top speed of 62 km/h, armour 8–12 mm thick, and a weight of 3.5 tons. Its dimensions were: 6.8 m in length, 2.25 m in width and 2.15 m in height

Sweden

Tidaholms M25, 1925. Built by the Tidaholms automobile firm in the mid-1920s, this 4.5-ton armoured car was of conventional design. It had a top speed of 45 km/h and was armed with a machine gun. Only two were built.

Tidaholms M26, 1926. The next Tidaholms model was similar to the first, but had different air louvres on the engine. After a single prototype had been produced, the armour was changed by facetting and two production models were built, one of which is seen here.

FM29 heavy armoured car, 1929 (*Below and below right*). The Landsverk firm dominated the armoured car field in Sweden from the late 1920s onwards, selling many models both at home and abroad. The FM29 was a five-man, 7.5-ton heavy armoured car, armed with a 37 mm gun in the front plate, a machine gun in the rear plate and another in an armoured jacket in the turret. The 4 × 4 vehicle had a top speed of 60 km/h and a range of 100 km. The symmetrical appearance was accentuated by the faceted armour plate. The car was 5.43 m long, 2.33 m wide, and 2.46 m high. The photograph at *right* shows the car from the rear.

FM31, 1931. This time, the car was open-topped and the 37 mm main armament was only protected by a gunshield. A machine gun was carried beside the driver. The six-man car was 3.3 m long, 5.4 m high, and 1.8 m wide, and weighed 4 tons. Its top speed was 60 km/h.

Landsverk 185, 1933 (*Above right*). Based on a Ford passenger car chassis, this four or five-man 4.2-ton light armoured car mounted a 20 mm gun and two machine guns. It had a top speed of 60 km/h and a range of 150 km. The car was 4.9 m long, 1.75 m wide, and 3.7 m high.

Lynx, 1938. The first model of the streamlined, very symmetrical 4 × 4 Lynx armoured car is shown. Weighing about 8 tons, it was designed with a 20 mm gun in the turret and a coaxial machine gun, plus further machine guns both front and rear.

Lynx, 1939 (*Below and right*). This purpose-built armoured car remained in service in the Swedish Army until 1950. It had a slightly larger turret than the earlier model, complete with a forward hinged cupola lid. Later modifications included an AA machine gun ring on the turret and the fitting of radio. With a top speed of 70 km/h and a range of 250 km, the six-man armoured car was 5.10 m (16 ft 9 ins) long, 2.28 m (7 ft 6½ ins) high, and 2.2 m (7 ft 2½ ins) wide.

Landsverk L180. The L180 used the Scania Vabis 6 × 4 truck chassis, with a front mounted engine and a conventional looking turret. Top speed was 80 km/h and range 288 kms. Main armament was a Madsen 20 mm cannon, with a coaxial machine gun. There was a second machine gun alongside the driver in the right-hand front plate.

Landsverk L182. The L180 was followed by two further models, the L181 and the L182, still basically the same, with a crew of 4 or 5 men, a weight of between 6 and 7 tons and a length of 5.6 m, a height of 3.88 m, and a width of 2.33 m.

L30 wheel-cum-track, 1931. Also known as the Strv fm/31, the L30 had the same turret as the M/31 light tank. It was not put into full production. On test it could switch from wheels to tracks, or vice versa, in under half a minute – even, it is claimed, when the AFV was moving! It weighed 11½ tons, had a top speed on wheels of 75 km/h, and 35 km/h on tracks, and a radius of action of 300 kms. Its main armament was a 37 mm gun, and the crew was four or five men.

Improvised armoured car. Scania-Vabis truck chassis were used for these improvised armoured cars, with an open-topped armoured chassis and pedestal-mounted cannon. The secondary armament comprised a machine gun alongside the driver.

USA

Scout car T1, 1928. Around 1928, the US Army started to use the Pontiac chassis as the basis of their scout cars, adding small amounts of armoured plate to the windscreen and radiator, and machine guns on pedestal mounts. The model seen here is the 1932 version, although the chassis is still basically the 1920s passenger car used earlier. Note the 'Chief Pontiac' sign above the radiator louvres. The scout car was 13 ft 9 ins long, 5 ft high and 6 ft 5 ins wide.

Scout car T1, 1928 (radio version). This version, photographed at the Aberdeen Proving Grounds (APG) in August 1932, was fitted for radio. It had a Type SCR-163A radio set plus a handcranked generator and was issued to the Cavalry and Field Artillery (Horsed), and to Divisional Signal Units.

Scout car T2, 1932 (*Below left*). The basis of this scout car was a 1932 Chevrolet Confederate series tourer, with armour added in much the same way as for the T1, putting the weight up to 2,970 lbs (about 450 lbs more than the T1). It was 14 ft long, 6 ft 5 ins wide, and 5 ft $10\frac{1}{2}$ ins high.

Cavalry School scout car, 1933. The gunner's fedora gives this 1933 Studebaker a gangster-like appearance! Note the long glacis plate covering the engine, and the very low, rear-mounted turret with a machine gun. It had all-round manual traverse and canvas mudguards to save weight.

T12 International scout car, 1935. This scout car used the C-series International truck chassis, with an open, five-seater, passenger car body and an armoured folding windscreen. It was 14 ft long, weighed 3,415 lbs, and had a top speed of 50 mph. This photograph was taken a couple of years later, when the large guard had been added to the front and the original tyres replaced by oversized Firestones.

A7SC4 scout car, 1935. Several of these A7SC4s were built by the Marmon-Herrington Company of Indianapolis, in 1935. They were all sold abroad, although the car was thoroughly tested by the US Army. Weighing 7,800 lbs and powered by an 85 hp Ford engine, it had a top speed of 75 mph.

Scout car T7, 1934. This was the first of a long line of scout cars to be built by the White Motor Company. Based on the $1\frac{1}{2}$-ton 4 × 4 Model truck chassis, it had a 75 hp engine and weighed 7,700 lbs. There were mounts for three .30 or .50 machine guns. The car later became known as the M1.

Command car T8. The hull armour on this version of the T7 scout car was raised, with vision slots, a pedestal-mounted .50 machine gun at the rear and a .30 machine gun on a ring mount at the front.

Scout car T9, 1935 (*Above and left*). Known also as the M2/M2E1, this 16 ft long, 7,900-lb car was developed by Corbit and Marmon-Herrington. It was built in Henderson, North Carolina, and was powered by a New Corbit Eight 94 hp engine, giving it a top speed of 50 mph. The M2E1 had slightly heavier axles and was fitted with a ring mount for a .50 machine gun, as the photograph at *left* shows.

T9 artillery car. This version of the T9 was modified to carry fire-control equipment for artillery use.

Scout car T13, 1937. Built by Marmon-Herrington, this 7,710-lb, 15 ft 10 in long car was based on the 1-ton Ford/Marmon-Herrington chassis and carried a .50 Browning M2 machine gun, on a skate ring.

Scout car M2A1, 1937. The final prototype for the M3, it was built by the White Motor Company. It had a 96 hp engine, weighed 7,810 lbs and was 16 ft 8 ins long.

Scout car M3, 1938. The final form of US Army World War 2 scout car began to emerge in the late 1930s, first with the M2A1 in 1937 and then the M3. Like other White scout cars, it had a skate type mount for the .50 heavy machine gun in front and a .30 at the rear side. Weighing 9,960 lbs, it could carry eight men, travel at 65 mph and had armour plate ranging from $\frac{1}{4}$–$\frac{1}{2}$ in thick. Range was 250 miles.

Scout car M3A1, 1939. First shown in 1939, the M3A1 was powered by a 110 hp engine, and proved to be both fast and reliable in service. Some 20,000 were built between 1940 and 1944. Many are still operational all over the world. The M3A1 weighed 8,616 lbs.

Scout car M3A1. Three views of the M3A1, showing its extreme versatility. Note, in the photograph *above*, the sprung roller bumper. In the *centre* photograph the car is towing a 37 mm anti-tank gun, while the photograph *below* shows it being used as an ambulance.

T1 light armored car, 1928 (*Above*). Basically, this was exactly the same car as the scout car, being a 1928 Pontiac with a little armour plate added. This particular car had folding seats at the rear and two .30 machine guns, one pedestal-mounted and one on a bracket dashboard mount. It was also known as the Armored car No. 6. It weighed only 2,600 lbs and had a cruising speed of 50 mph.

T2 armored car, 1929 (*Top right*). La Salle built the T2 armored car in 1928 and during the following years various models (modified), were produced. Seen here are the T2E1 and T2E2. The T2E1 (on the *left*, No. 1303) had a turret made up of plates bolted on to a traversable ring and containing a .30 machine gun. The car also

had sloping armour plate $\frac{1}{8}$ in thick, putting its weight up to 6,000 lbs (the original T2 had weighed some 4,850 lbs). The T2E2 (on the *right*, No. 1300) had the armour behind the driver's compartment lowered, with taller plates being used for the open turret.

T2E2 armored car, 1930 (*Above*). Another photograph of the T2E2, with a good view of the turret. The next model, T2E3, had an even lower silhouette, primarily by having smaller plates on the turret.

T7 armored car, 1930 (*Below, right and above right*). Built by the Quartermaster Corps. The T7 had a water-cooled .30 Browning machine gun in the turret and an air-cooled Browning in the front plate. Its road speed was 60 mph, weight 7,200 lbs and length 14 ft. Mudguards were added later.

Christie Airborne Combat Car, 1933 (*Above and right*). The brilliant, but eccentric, J. Walter Christie, seen here in the turret of his wheeled armored car, is probably better known for his tracked and wheel-cum-track vehicles. However, he also designed this 2.2-ton car, which had a crew of two and was powered by a 250 hp engine producing a top speed cross-country of 35 mph and on roads a staggering 110 mph! Dimensions were: length, 14 ft 2 ins; width, 6 ft; and height, 7 ft.

TK5, 1933. Built by Marmon-Herrington, this was a very conventional looking armoured car. Note the spare wheel in an armoured box on the side, and the conical turret with machine gun. Dimensions were: length 17 ft 2 ins; width, 7 ft 6½ ins; and height, 8 ft.

TK5 (TH31OALF-1). This model had the Swedish Landsverk turret fitted, mounting a 37 mm gun and coaxial machine gun. It was built to sell to Persia.

TK6, 1933. Built by La Salle, also for sale to Persia, in 1933. These 10.4-ton armoured cars had a top speed of 52 mph, and 23 mph in reverse. A large and cumbersome vehicle, it mounted a 37 mm and a coaxial .30 machine gun in the turret, plus a further .30 to the right of the driver. None were purchased by the US Army.

T11 armored car, 1933. Specifications for the T11 were laid down by the Ordnance Corps in 1932. The Four-Wheel Drive Auto Company (FWD) built the prototype, but Marmon-Herrington got the contract for the production models, resulting in quite a scandal as Marmon-Herrington's bid was well below the actual cost of building the cars. In consequence, FWD, who had built hundreds of heavy trucks for the Army in the late 1920s/early 1930s, did not bid for another Army contract for some years. The T11 weighed about 11,250 lbs and had a four-man crew.

T11E1 armored car, 1934. The weight of this model went up to 14,000 lbs. Note the machine gun ball mounting in the front glacis. Various changes were made to the turret, and the engine was uprated to 118 hp.

T11E2 armored car, 1934. This model had a completely new turret, mounting both .50 and .30 machine guns, plus a second .30 in the front plate. Rear hull was altered to accommodate a 110 hp Hercules engine which gave the 12,800-lb car a top speed of 48 mph. Marmon-Herrington built six of these cars.

Tucker Tiger armored car, 1938 (*Above left*). This very fast little armoured car ($13\frac{1}{2}$ ft long and 8 ft high) was called the Tucker Tiger Tank, which of course it was not! It had a 175 hp engine which Tucker claimed gave it a top speed of 100 mph, although the US Army said 74 mph. Note the plastic-domed turret which mounted a 37 mm gun, plus three machine guns in the hull.

T4 6 × 4 armored car, 1932 (*Above*). This multi-wheel armoured car was built by the James Cunningham Company and powered by their V8 engine, which produced 133 hp. The turret had all-round traverse and mounted both .50 and .30 machine guns. It weighed 9,800 lbs and had a cruising speed of 55 mph.

M1 armored car, 1932 (*Left*). The T4 was standardised as the M1 armored car, with conventional headlamps replacing the bullet-shaped ones of the prototype. Nearly 16 ft long, the armour thickness varied between $\frac{3}{16}$ in to $\frac{1}{2}$ in.

Trackless Tank, 1940 (*Above and left*). Built by the Trackless Tank Corporation and tested at the Aberdeen Proving Grounds in early 1941. It had chain drive to the three back axles, while steering was only to the front axle. It was powered by a 270 hp Guiberson diesel engine and was a 'one only'. Later in 1941, the T13 was produced, which owed a great deal to the Trackless Tank.

South America

Mexico: Fiat armoured car, 1929. Although Pancho Villa's forces had an improvised armoured car during the revolutionary days of 1914, no armoured car was seen in Mexico until the 1929 revolution. The car in question was this Fiat, with an open-topped body, containing a pedestal-mounted machine gun, with an armoured shield.

Guatemala: FWD lorry. It is interesting to see one of the hundreds of lorries built by the Four-Wheel Drive Auto Company of the USA being used in South America as an improvised armoured car. Note the high, box hull, with two water-cooled .50 Browning machine guns on pedestal mounts.

Venezuela: Tortuga armoured car, 1934. Based on the Ford 6 × 4 chassis, these strange looking armoured cars mounted a Hotchkiss machine gun in their domed turrets.

Brazil: White scout car, 1942. Motorised troops of the Brazilian Army parade shortly after Brazil's declaration of war against Germany on 22 August 1942. The vehicles are American M3A1 scout cars.

4 World War Two

The success of the German *Blitzkrieg* tactics rocketed armoured cars back into favour, in particular with the British, and they began producing a startling array of different models – Guy, Humber, Daimler, AEC, Coventry, Thorneycroft, Morris, Foden, the list is never ending. Armoured cars really came into their own in the vast open spaces of the Western Desert, establishing their main wartime role of medium reconnaissance as the task for which they were ideally suited. Patrols of armoured cars were able to operate over long distances, independently and self-contained, with growing expertise that rapidly gained them an enviable reputation as the eyes and ears of the formation commander. But of course, they were much too versatile to be used just for medium reconnaissance. They were ideal for guarding open flanks or setting up screens, for mobile patrolling or raiding deep into enemy territory, as well as for the more mundane tasks of convoy protection and liaison. All now had adequate long range radio communications, so they were able to get their information back to the commander quickly enough for it to be of real value.

Armoured cars did not have things all their own way. They were vulnerable to enemy fire, especially from medium or heavy tanks and anti-tank guns. When the near-perfect conditions of North Africa were exchanged for the more varied and closer country of Europe, their job became far more hazardous. Their popularity waned and some of their roles had to be taken over by other arms. For example, the job of close, battlefield recce had in future to be performed by tanks which were capable of fighting for their information rather than relying upon stealth. On rare occasions, armoured cars did get the opportunity to show their worth, for example by locating a vital unguarded crossing over a major obstacle, and then holding it until the main forces could catch up with these 'Greyhounds of the battlefield'.

Their multiplicity of roles dictated the need for balanced grouping within the armoured car regiment, rather than just armoured cars operating on their own. There had always been a need for the smaller scout cars, which could move faster and less obtrusively than the larger armoured cars, but still needed the firepower of the armoured cars to overwatch them and be there to get them out of trouble. Still heavier supporting weapons were also needed, together with a dismounted element to take on foot recces, the guarding armoured car leaguers, minelaying and basic engineering tasks, so the armoured car regiment grew into a complex all-purpose unit, which was capable of carrying out all its wide ranging tasks. As the German Army retreated back into the Fatherland and operations became more mobile, the British, at least, made more use of their armoured cars. Russia on the other hand, which had built only one new type of small armoured car during the whole of the war, did not attempt to replace their large numbers of prewar-built cars knocked out by the Germans in the early days of *Barbarossa*. The Germans themselves replaced their lighter armoured cars with more versatile half-tracks, but their heavier models continued in production right up to the end. Perhaps the most interesting nation was America, which produced many armoured cars and scout cars for others to use, such as the Staghound for the British, but themselves used only the M8 Greyhound, and that in no great numbers.

At the end of World War 2 armoured cars had a very mixed record. They clearly did not emerge as an arm of decision as did the tank. However, as in World War 1, they had proved their versatility, adaptability and general usefulness. This was to stand them in good stead in the early days of peace, when they were once again to be used as 'maids of all work' for worldwide internal security and policing roles.

M8 Greyhound, 1943. A US Army reconnaissance car rolls through Kinzweiter, Germany on the road to Geilenkirchen, an important Siegfried Line strongpoint, in November 1944. The fast M8 was an ideal recce vehicle and was the US Army's most used armoured car of the war. At left, in a ditch is a knocked-out German StuG assault gun.

4 WORLD WAR TWO
Great Britain

Alvis scout car, Dingo (*Top right and right*). In 1938, the Mechanisation Board invited three firms to submit prototypes to meet specifications which the Board had laid down for a new class of light armoured turretless vehicles, to be used for scouting purposes. One of these firms was Alvis Ltd of Coventry and their model was known as the 'Dingo'. Like the others, it was a two-man vehicle, with a single Bren light machine gun, weighing about 2 tons and with armour up to 14 mm thick. The Dingo proved to be a good performer, especially cross-country. Note the rear-mounted engine. It is interesting to see that the name 'Dingo' was used during World War 2 as the generic name for all scout cars, despite the fact that the Alvis scout car design was dropped by the War Office.

Alvis scout car. Another version from Alvis, which was almost identical, except that the top armour sloped inwards.

BSA scout car, 1937. The other main contender was built by BSA Cycles Ltd of Birmingham. It was also a two-man, four-wheel drive vehicle with independent suspension. It weighed half a ton more than the Dingo, and had a marginally inferior performance. However, it was cheaper, and it had a lower centre of gravity than the Dingo which proved the clinchers after the War Office decided that all scout cars must be fully armoured, including a roof. The BSA design was therefore chosen. In fact, it went on to do very well, covering 10,000 miles during further trials, without any major defects. The hull was then redesigned and a roof added. The final design was then taken over by the Daimler Company.

Daimler scout car Mark 1, 1939. The first order for scout cars Mark 1 was placed in 1939 and was for 172 of these splendid little vehicles, which gave excellent service in all theatres throughout the war. The weight was now 2.8 tons, and the 55 hp Daimler 6-cylinder engine gave it a top speed of 55–60 mph. The car had a range of 200 miles. It was 10 ft 5 ins long, 5 ft 7½ ins wide, and 4 ft 11 ins high.

Daimler scout car Mark 1a (*Below left*). The only difference between the Mark 1a and the Mark 1 was that the Mark 1a was fitted with a folding, instead of a sliding, roof. Some 6,626 Daimler scout cars of all marks were produced during the war.

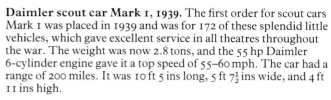

Daimler scout car Mark 1b. The designation Mark 1b indicated that, in addition to the the introduction of the folding roof, the fan draught for the engine was reversed. This Mark 1b belonged to the 7th Armoured Division in the Western Desert in 1942. It has been locally modified by fixing a plate between the front and rear mudguards, thus forming a large and capacious stowage bin.

Daimler scout car, Mark III. The four-wheel steering on the Mark I was found to be a liability for unskilled drivers, so it was dropped with the Mark II. The last version, the Mark III, seen here, weighed 3.15 tons, had a fully waterproofed engine and the roof removed.

Humber scout car, Mark I. So great was the demand for scout cars that other firms had to be asked to produce them, including the Rootes Group, which produced the Humber. Slightly heavier (3.39 tons) and larger (12 ft 7 ins long, 6 ft 2½ ins wide, 6 ft 11½ ins high) it had the same general layout as the Daimler, but could carry three men. It had a top speed of 60 mph and a range of 200 miles.

Beaverette Mark I, light reconnaissance car, 1941 (*Above left*). Known also as the Standard Car 4 × 2, and (by the RAF) as the Car, Armoured, Light Standard Type C Beaverette I, this 2-ton, lightly armoured car, was produced at the instigation of Lord Beaverbrook for the defence of airfields and aircraft factories. It was $13\frac{1}{2}$ ft long, 5 ft 3 ins wide, and 5 ft high and it had a top speed of 40 mph.

Beaverette Mark II (*Above*). The main difference between this Mark and the Mark I was that the 11 mm armour was continued all the way round – the rear of the Mark I had been protected only by 3-in oak planks, such was the situation in Britain, after the Dunkirk evacuation.

Beaverette Mark III. The 'Beaverbug', as it was also called, weighed 2.6 tons, had better armour plate and a small turret with a hinged lid, although it was sometimes open at the front, as shown in the photograph. A Mark IV was also produced, and in all 2,800 Beaverettes were manufactured for home defence purposes by the Army and RAF. The Beaverette in the photograph was in RAF use, being armed with twin Vickers 'K' aircraft-type machine guns, and was used for airfield defence.

Humber Mark I, Ironside I, light reconnaissance car. Built on the chassis of a normal Humber Super Snipe, but with War Department wheels, runflat tyres and other minor changes. Three of these cars were specially modified for use by the Royal Family and Cabinet Ministers, and were called 'Special Ironsides Saloons'. The Humber Mark I weighed 2.8 tons, had armour 12 mm thick and a top speed of 45 mph. It was 14 ft 4 ins long.

Humber Mark II light reconnaissance car (*Above and above right*). This model was similar to the Ironside I, but with roof armour and a small open-topped turret, which put the weight up to just under 3 tons. As the photographs show, the armament was a Boys .55 in anti-tank rifle and a Bren gun. Crew was three men.

Humber Mark III, 1941 (*Left*). This model had four-wheel drive. Over 3,600 of all Marks were built during the war and saw service abroad as well as in the UK. They were mainly used by recce regiments in infantry divisions and by the RAF Regiment.

Hillman Gnat, 1942 (*Below*). This tiny two-man light recce car was built in prototype form only. The intention was that it would take over from unarmoured motor cycle combinations, armed with Bren guns, which were in service in fair numbers in 1940–41. The Gnat had a poor cross-country performance, being underpowered, and the project soon lapsed.

Morris Mark I light reconnaissance car, 1941 (*Left*). Yet another recce car built in large numbers was produced by Morris Motors Ltd. It was a 4 × 2 car which weighed 3.7 tons and was powered by a 72 bhp engine. With a crew of three, the car was 13 ft 3½ ins long, 6 ft 8 ins wide, and 6 ft 2 ins high, had a top speed of 50 mph and armour 14 mm thick.

Morris Mark II. The Mark II model had four-wheel drive and leaf-spring suspension. As the photograph shows, the armament was a Boys anti-tank rifle and a Bren gun. Total production of Morris light reconnaissance cars was about 2,200.

Morris experimental tank. Similar to the Morris Mark II, but with two turrets, it was not put into production.

Buick Home Guard armoured car. In 1940, many improvised armoured cars were built all over UK for use with the Home Guard, in the event of an invasion. This particular car, a Buick, was presented to the West Farleigh Home Guard (near Maidstone, Kent) and is seen here being fitted with its armour.

Rolls-Royce Home Guard armoured car. Built by Council Workshops for the London County Council Battalion of the Home Guard, this 20 hp Rolls saloon car had a fully traversing turret mounting a Vickers machine gun and carried a crew of three.

Sunbeam Home Guard armoured car. This 'Tickler Tank' was the brainchild of Colonel Tickler of Maidenhead and had sheets of metal, rescued from rubbish dumps, fixed around the car chassis! War workers give the crew a cheery send off.

Sunbeam Home Guard armoured car. The object of this photograph was to show how the Home Guard would deal with enemy armoured cars – 'the raider rumbles along a country lane, but all the time, British troops knowing the country and every little bump in it, are closing in to an ambush!'

Bentley Home Guard armoured car. The Herts Home Guard were the lucky owners of this well armoured Bentley, presented by Mrs John Appleton, wife of a local businessman, on 28 July 1940.

General Motors Home Guard armoured car. Even the Prime Minister himself took a great interest in the improvised armoured cars. This one belonged to the 1st American Squadron of the Home Guard, and was photographed on Horseguards Parade on 9 January 1941.

Bedford anti-tank lorry, 1941. Many different types of Bedford lorry were impressed into military service and hastily armoured with boiler-plate. They carried a variety of weapons and were to be used against the German invaders when they landed. This 30-cwt armoured anti-tank Bedford OXA was one of the early ones, but there were many others – such as the Armadillo I, II and III.

Rolls-Royce armoured car, 1940. The splendid old 1920 and 1924 pattern Rolls were still in service at the start of World War 2, mostly being used for training in the UK, although some of them were in the Middle East. The first armoured car regiment of 7th Armoured Dvision – the 11th Hussars – was equipped with 1924 pattern cars, modernised by replacing the existing turret with an open-topped version mounting a Boys anti-tank rifle, a Bren light machine gun and a smoke discharger. They saw active service against the Italians in Cyrenaica in 1940–41. The photograph *below* was taken at 'The Wire' along the Egyptian border, while the photograph *below right* shows a Cherry Picker patrol approaching Bardia.

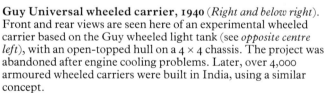

Guy Universal wheeled carrier, 1940 (*Right and below right*). Front and rear views are seen here of an experimental wheeled carrier based on the Guy wheeled light tank (see *opposite centre left*), with an open-topped hull on a 4 × 4 chassis. The project was abandoned after engine cooling problems. Later, over 4,000 armoured wheeled carriers were built in India, using a similar concept.

134

Guy Quad armoured car (experimental), 1938. The original design for the Guy armoured car was based on the Guy Quad-Ant artillery tractor chassis. Five mild steel prototypes were built in 1938 by Guy Motors Ltd, and were of rivetted construction.

Guy armoured car Mark I, 1939. Trials with the Guy Quad were most successful, but, before going ahead with production, the firm asked if they could use a welding process for fabricating the hulls and turrets. The War Office agreed and a rotary manipulator and jigs were designed by Guy Motors. Production started in 1939 and 101 Guy armoured cars – also known as the Guy Wheeled Light Tank – were built *in toto*, the first welded armoured cars ever to be produced for the British Army. The initial batch mounted one .5 and one .303 Vickers machine guns, but the last 51 had Besa machine guns (one 15 mm and one 7.92 mm) and were designated Mark IA. The three-man armoured car weighed 5.75 tons, and had a top speed of 35 mph and a range of 210 miles. It was $13\frac{1}{2}$ ft long, $6\frac{2}{3}$ ft wide, and $7\frac{1}{2}$ ft high. The armour was 15 mm maximum. A troop of four Guy armoured cars belonging to 12L was used as a mobile guard for the Royal family from 1940–42. Two of these cars were also put at the disposal of the Cabinet and Churchill used one of them to tour London during some of the heaviest air raids to comfort survivors and encourage Civil Defence volunteers.

Humber Mark I armoured car, 1940. The lion's share of the armoured cars in British production during World War 2 were built by Rootes Group. Most of these were Humbers which saw service all over the world from 1941. Closely modelled on the Guy armoured car, and taking as the basis the chassis of the Karrier KT4 artillery tractor as supplied to the Indian Army pre-war, the first production contract, for 500, was awarded in 1940. Weighing 6.85 tons, the Mark I had a crew of three, a top speed of 45 mph and a range of 250 miles. Dimensions were : length 15 ft; width, 7 ft 2 ins; and height, 7 ft 10 ins.

Humber Mark II, 1941. The Mark II had a redesigned front hull, with the driver's visor built into the front plate and the radiator armour altered at the rear. Armament was still one 15 mm Besa and one 7.92 mm Besa. Its weight was up by about a quarter ton.

Humber Mark III, 1942. Although it still weighed 7.1 tons, the Mark III had a more roomy turret, which enabled the crew to be increased to four men.

Humber Mark IV (*Above right*). Last of the Humber line to be built, it mounted the American 37 mm gun as its main armament – the first British vehicle to do so. Secondary armament remained a 7.92 mm Besa, and the crew was reduced to three men.

Humber AA Mark I, 1942. On this model, the normal turret has been removed and replaced with a specially designed one equipped with four Besa 7.92 mm machine guns and an AA ring sight.

Daimler Mark I armoured car, 1940. The design of the 4 × 4 welded, 6.8-ton armoured car was based on the Daimler scout car and was in all intents and purposes just a larger edition with a turret. The main armament was a 2-pdr gun, with a coaxially-mounted Besa 7.92 mm machine gun. The 6-cylinder, 95 bhp Daimler engine gave the car a top speed of 50 mph. It had a range of 200 miles, when an auxiliary fuel tank was carried. It was 13 ft long, 8 ft wide, and 7 ft 4 ins high.

Daimler Mark II. The Mark II incorporated various modifications, including an improved turret, driver's escape hatch, modified gun mounting and a different radiator. Nearly 2,700 Daimlers were built during World War 2 and the type saw service in most theatres of war. The armour was 16 mm thick. It had a crew of three. Some were modified for use as regimental command vehicles; these had their turrets removed.

Daimler with wading equipment (*Above right*). General view of a Daimler fitted with wading equipment, including a gun apron, radiator duct and flap valve on the exhaust, which was submerged during the wade.

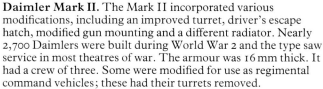

AEC Mark I heavy armoured car, 1941. Although the armoured car had rapidly taken over the role of the light tank it was initially equipped only with machine guns and was thus no match for enemy armour. Consequently, it became the fashion to mount various captured weapons of 20 mm calibre and upwards on armoured car chassis in order to produce a support weapon that could deal with enemy light armour. This need for a heavy armoured car was taken up by the Associated Equipment Company Ltd (AEC) as a private venture and they managed to win a production order by introducing a mock-up of their heavy armoured car onto Horse Guards Parade during a vehicle demonstration given to the Prime Minister in 1941. Weighing 11 tons, the Mark I had basically the same turret as on the Valentine tank, which mounted a 2-pdr gun as its main armament.

AEC Mark II. At 12.7 tons, the Mark II was even heavier than the Mark I. It mounted a 6-pdr gun plus a Besa machine gun, and also had a more powerful engine – an AEC diesel 158 bhp which increased the top speed to 41 mph. The front hull was redesigned to give better protection (the armour was 30 mm thick). Dimensions were: length, 17 ft; height, 8 ft 10 ins; and width, 8 ft 10 ins.

AEC Mark III. Externally, the only difference from the Mark II on the Mark III was the replacement of the 6-pdr with a 75 mm gun, which gave this heavy armoured car comparable gunpower to many medium tanks. A total of 629 AECs was built, and the cars saw service mainly in the Heavy Troops of armoured car squadrons, providing support to lighter and more lightly armed cars.

AEC AA, 1944 (*Below*). Last of the British wartime AA developments on a wheeled chassis was the AEC AA, which utilised a Mark II armoured car chassis with a Crusader AA II tank turret mounting twin 20 mm Oerlikon guns. It was not put into production because the Allies achieved virtual domination in the air over Europe from the Normandy landings onwards.

Coventry Mark I armoured car, 1944. This car was produced as a combined effort by Humber Ltd, Commer Cars Ltd and Daimler Company Ltd, the aim being to produce a standard armoured car to replace both the Humber and Daimler armoured cars. Its design owes more to the Daimler, but it was powered by an American engine – a 175 bhp, 6-cylinder Hercules RXLO. It had duplicate driving controls for driving backwards and mounted a 2-pdr and coaxial Besa machine gun. The 11½-ton car had a crew of four and armour 14 mm thick. Its dimensions were: length (excluding gun), 15 ft 6½ ins, width, 8 ft 9 ins; and height; 7 ft 9 ins.

Coventry Mark III armoured car. Although substantial orders were placed, the war ended before many Coventry armoured cars were produced. The Mark II mounted a 75 mm gun instead of the 2-pdr, the crew being reduced to three. The Mark III was an improved Mark II and would undoubtedly have been a formidable armoured car. The Coventry saw no action in World War 2.

Staghound Mark III armoured car. The Staghound was an American-produced armoured car, so it is covered in full in Part 4, Section 11 (pages 175 to 179). However, as it was built basically for the British, it is worth including here one interesting modification to the original American Staghound, the fitting of a Crusader tank turret mounting a 75 mm gun with a coaxial Besa machine gun.

AEC Deacon gun carrier, 1942. A rudimentary self-propelled gun, the Deacon mounted a 6-pdr gun in a flat-sided turret on an AEC Matador 4 × 4 chassis. The 175 built were rushed out to the Middle East to bolster up anti-tank batteries. They saw service until the end of the North African campaign and were then handed over to the Turks. The 12-ton Deacon had a top speed of 20 mph.

Thornycroft gun carrier, 1942. A 17-pdr gun was rear-mounted on this 13.75-ton gun carrier. The end of the barrel is just visible in this front view photograph. It proved to have a poor cross-country performance, so, despite promising gunnery trials, the project was dropped.

Foden gun carrier. An early wartime adaptation was the mounting of a 4-inch naval gun on to a 6 × 4 Foden lorry, mainly for coastal defence purposes.

Morris AA gun carrier. Designed for use in protecting road convoys was this 40 mm Bofors AA gun mounted on a Morris lorry.

Miscellaneous gun carriers. Three further adaptations are shown on this page. The first (*right*), used by the LRDG, consists of machine guns mounted on a lorry; the second (*below*) is a 2-pdr anti-tank gun being carried *portée* and fired from the back of the lorry, while the third (*bottom*) is a 25 mm being used by the Arab Legion in Transjordan. 25-pdrs were used in 'Jock' Columns in the early days of the Western Desert in the anti-tank role in much the same way.

Miscellaneous armed jeeps. The ubiquitous Jeep was often armed with a variety of weapons for use with such fast moving outfits as the Long Range Desert Group, Popski's Private Army and the like. In the four photographs on this page, .50 Brownings, .30 Brownings, aircraft machine guns, etc., are all used to provide impressive firepower, but no armour was fitted in order not to reduce mobility.

General Motors Coupe. This GM 4 × 4 15-cwt was fitted with a symmetrical-looking, armoured body, probably for command use.

Armoured Command Vehicle AEC 4 × 4, Mark I (*Below right*). Mobile warfare demands mobile, protected command posts, especially for senior officers of armoured formations and their staff. They must be large enough to carry all the impedimenta of such an headquarters – radios, maps, plans, staff tables, etc. After various *ad hoc* versions, a proper design was produced, built on the AEC Matador chassis. There were two versions, HP (High Power) and LP (Low Power), the former mounting more powerful radio sets. Both were used all over the world from 1941 onwards. Three were captured by Rommel and used subsequently by him (see Part 4, page 158).

Interior of an ACV (*Below*). General view inside an ACV (4 × 4), showing a typical layout, but without all the maps, office paraphernalia or staff.

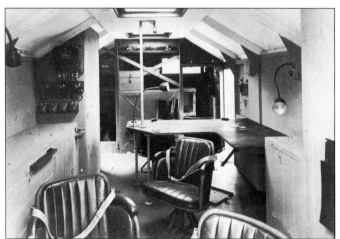

Armoured Command Vehicle AEC 6 × 6, Mark I. Later in the war, a new ACV, larger than the AEC 4 × 4, was produced, this time on an AEC 6 × 6 chassis with a 150 bhp diesel engine, whereas the previous version had a 95 bhp diesel. Again, there were HP and LP versions.

Commonwealth

Australia: Scout car 4 × 4, 1942. This small turretless car of simple design had a crew of two. The sides were vertical and the rear deck sloped quite sharply. It was 15 ft long, 6 ft 10 ins wide, and 6 ft 1 in high.

Australia: Rover car, 1943. Another turretless, squat car with an open top and covered rear wheels. Production vehicles were shorter than the original prototype which was 20 ft 1 in long, 7 ft 7 ins wide, and 7 ft high.

Australia: Rhino armoured car, 1943. The only wartime-built Australian armoured car, with a turret resembling that of a British Crusader in shape and mounting a 2-pdr gun, the Rhino's hull was not unlike that of a Daimler armoured car. Note the three diagonal bullet deflectors on the front glacis plate.

Australia: Utility car, 1943. A number of the 4 × 4 scout cars were converted into armoured cargo vehicles for use by the American forces in the Pacific theatre.

Canada: Ford 1 Lynx 1 scout car. Built by the Ford Motor Company of Canada, this was the Canadian version of the Daimler scout car, but it was larger (1 ft 8½ ins longer) and one ton heavier. The engine was a Ford V8 95 bhp, which gave the car a top speed of 57 mph. Its armour was 30 mm thick, and the Lynx car had a range of 200 miles.

Canada: Ford 2 Lynx 2 scout car. The Mark II incorporated a number of modifications, including strengthened chassis components (springs and axles) and no armoured roof. Over 3,000 Lynx were built in Canada during World War 2. Dimensions were: length, 12 ft 1½ in; width, 6 ft 1 in; and height, 5 ft 10 ins.

Canada: GM Mark I Otter 1 light reconnaissance car (*Above left*). The Canadian-produced version of the Humber III light reconnaissance car, it used mainly Canadian components and a GM 104 bhp engine. Between 1942 and 1945, the Canadians built over 1,700, which were used mainly by Canadian troops in Italy, although some were supplied to the British Army and the RAF Regiment. The cars operated by the latter were armed with a 20 mm cannon and twin AA Browning machine guns. The Otter weighed 4.8 tons, had a crew of three and was 14 ft 9 ins long, 7 ft wide, and 8 ft high.

Canada: GM Mark I Fox I armoured car, 1942 (*Above*). Some 200 of this Canadian-built version of the Humber III were produced, armed with both a heavy and a light Browning machine gun instead of the Besas. A Mark II Fox was also produced, equivalent to the Humber IV.

Canada: GM armoured personnel carrier. General Motors of Canada produced a small APC based on a 15-cwt 4 × 4 truck.

India: India Pattern Mark II armoured carrier, 1942. There were a large number of different armoured wheeled carriers built in India during World War 2. The first production model was known as the Armoured Carrier, Wheeled, IP Mark I and was based on the Guy Universal Wheeled Carrier (see Part 4, Section 1, page 134). The Mark II and all subsequent models were based on the Ford 4 × 4 chassis supplied from Canada. The vehicle was turretless, but was armed with a Boys anti-tank rifle and a Bren gun on an AA mount. The photograph shows the Mark IIA which had slightly larger tyres than the Mark II.

South Africa: Marmon-Herrington Mark I armoured car, 1940. The Union of South Africa built an excellent series of armoured cars during World War 2, many of which saw much service in the Western Desert. The basis of the car was a conventional 4 × 2 Ford 3-ton chassis, armoured by the South African Iron and Steel Corporation, with Marmon Herrington conversion to four-wheel drive for the Mark II onwards. After exhaustive trials, the prototype was accepted for production in January 1940, the initial order being increased to 1,000 after the war spread to North Africa. The entire resources of South Africa had to be co-ordinated to produce cars in quantity, but all the weapons came from Great Britain. The Mark I mounted a Vickers water-cooled machine gun in a ball mounting in the circular turret and another in the left-hand side of the hull. Some models were rivetted, others welded. The crew was four and the length of the wheelbase of the Mark I was 11 ft 2 ins. Some 110 plus of the 4 × 2 version were built. Note how the armour extends down in front of the front wheels.

South Africa: Marmon-Herrington Mark II, 1940. The Mark II had a longer and stronger wheelbase, a longer bonnet and four-wheel drive. The front mudguards were also redesigned, as the photograph, taken during a 'Unite for Victory' parade in Johannesburg, shows. The first cars were handed over to the South African armoured car companies in May 1940 (Mk I) and November 1940 (Mk II) and initially saw service against the Italians in East Africa. The War Office then asked South Africa to supply cars for British Army use in the Western Desert.

South Africa: Marmon-Herrington conversions (*Right and below right*). The cars supplied to the British were equipped to contemporary War Office standards, with a Boys anti-tank rifle and Bren light machine gun, plus a second Bren (AA) and a rear-mounted Vickers machine gun. However, many were converted by using captured weapons to improve their firepower. The *top right* photograph shows an Italian Breda 20 mm cannon being employed against dive bombers during the siege of Tobruk, while the *bottom right* mounts an Italian 47 mm anti-tank gun.

South Africa: Marmon-Herrington Mark III, 1941 (*Below*). The demand for armoured cars grew and, in mid-1941, the Mark III took its place on the production lines. It still used the Ford chassis but with a wheelbase of only 9 ft 9 ins. The round turret had been replaced by an octagonal one, with a Boys anti-tank rifle and two machine guns, one for AA use. The photograph, taken in East Africa, shows a rather battered car which had just won a duel with an enemy field gun. Over 2,600 Mark IIIs were built for the Union Defence force (UDF) and the War Office, the last being delivered in August 1942. Its dimensions were: length, 17 ft 5 ins; width, 7 ft 6½ ins; and height 8 ft 2½ ins. Again, there were many conversions, with a wide variety of captured weapons being fitted, including Italian 47 mm, German 37 mm and French 25 mm anti-tank guns.

South Africa: Marmon-Herrington Mark IV, 1942. As the photograph shows, the Mark IV was a completely redesigned armoured car, mounting as its main weapon a 2-pdr gun. Basic components remained the same, but the armoured hull now took the place of the chassis. Initially, there was no mounting for a coaxial machine gun, but, later, first a Vickers and then a Browning (seen here) was fitted and coupled coaxially. A second Browning (first .50, then .30) was carried on the turret roof on an AA mounting. Over 2,000 Mark IVs were built. As well as the four basic Marks there were others which did not reach full production, including an eight-wheeler (Mk VI), which was ordered in mid-1942 but later cancelled. The Mark IV went on in service all over the world after the war. Its dimensions were: length, 15 ft; width, 6 ft; and height, 7 ft.

Belgium

Ford 91Y, 1939. This partly armoured vehicle had four-wheel drive and was used for a variety of purposes. Those not destroyed during the invasion were used later by the Germans.

Berliet VUDB, 1930. The only modern armoured cars in the Belgian Army at the start of World War 2 were a number of French Berliet purchased in the early 1930s. Twelve of these armoured troop carriers were among the AFVs bought.

Denmark

Holger-Danske V3, 1945. The Holger-Danske section of the Danish Resistance made this improvised armoured car in 1945 and used it to support their attacks on factories collaborating with the Germans. It was a Ford lorry chassis with metal plates attached. It was called the V3 as a joke, because the Germans were then using their V1 and V2 rockets against the British

France

Panhard 178B. At the end of World War 2, the French equipped their Panhard 178 with a new, cast and welded turret which put the weight up by 500 lbs, but did not materially affect the car's mobility. The new turret mounted a 47 mm cannon and a 7.5 mm machine gun. This car was later used in Syria, Indo-China and elsewhere abroad.

Bedford 15-cwt with 20 mm anti-tank gun (*Below*). Two 25 mm 34SA guns, manned by Free French Forces in Libya, being carried in British 15-cwts.

Laffly with 25 mm anti-tank gun (*Above*). Seen in France soon after the outbreak of World War 2 is a six-wheel Laffly carrying *portée* a 25 mm anti-tank gun, known as the 34SA. The standard light infantry anti-tank gun in the French Army, the 34SA had a very limited range and poor penetrative power.

Laffly with MG Mle 1931. This six-wheel Laffly in Southern Tunisia has twin Mle 1931 machine guns (7.5 mm, with their distinctive 150 round magazines).

Laffly 80AM automitrailleuse de Decouverte. Two Laffly Vincennes, as they were also called, motor past General de Gaulle in North Africa in 1943. (See Part 3, page 79 for a description of the armoured car.)

CDM improvised armoured car, 1943. Secretly constructed by the French Resistance and then hidden to await the Allied invasion, the CDM (Camouflage du Matériel) used a GMC lorry chassis, armoured and equipped with the turrets of Panhard armoured cars. They mounted various weapons, ranging from 13.6 mm to 47 mm guns.

La Rochelle Mini, 1945. Photographed between two larger improvised armoured cars are two little one-man armoured cars. They used a Simca chassis and mounted one machine gun. They were built by the Resistance.

La Rochelle improvised armoured car, 1945. A selection of three views of two more improvised armoured cars built by the Resistance using lorry chassis and mounting two machine guns, one in the squat turret, the other in the front plate. They were used against the retreating German forces and were normally clearly marked with a large French air force roundel on the bonnet, as ground-to-air recognition symbols.

Germany

SdKfz221 leichter panzerspähwagen, 1935. Issued to the scout squadrons of reconnaissance detachments in both panzer and motorised infantry divisions, this 4-ton, two-man scout car saw service throughout the war. Some 340 were produced between 1935 and 1940. It was armed with a single MG34, and had a top speed of 90 km/h and a range of 320 km. It was 4.8 m long, 1.95 m wide, and 1.7 m high.

SdKfz221 mit 2.8 cm gun, 1942 (*Below*). The early 221s had to be accompanied by an armoured car with the firepower to provide covering fire. However, from 1942, the 221 was itself fitted with a 2.8 cm sPzB41 gun, which had a tapered bore, from 2.8 cm at the breech end down to 2 cm at the muzzle. The turret had to be altered and the MG34 machine gun removed to make way for the larger weapon. Some earlier cars had been equipped with an anti-tank rifle in addition to the MG34, but only a few of these conversions were carried out.

SdKfz222 leichter panzerspähwagen, 1936 (*Above and left*). About 1,000 of these three-man, 4.8-ton cars were produced between 1936 and 1943. It mounted a 2 cm gun plus a coaxial MG34 and was to be found mainly in the recce companies of tank battalions. The photographs of this early model show the anti-grenade mesh screen on the turret very clearly. It was split down the middle and could be folded outwards (photograph *left*). The car was 4.8 m long, 1.95 m wide, and 2 m high. Later vehicles had heavier gun mounts which enabled both the 2 cm and machine gun to be elevated almost vertically and thus used for AA protection, as the *left* photograph also shows.

SdKfz 223 leichter panzerspähwagen (funkwagen), 1935 (*Opposite*). This was a wireless car which mounted a long-range radio set and had a frame aerial around the hull. It was very similar to the SdKfz 222, but with a smaller turret mounting only an MG34. The turret was nine-sided and had a hinged anti-grenade mesh screen. Weighing 4.4 tons, and with a three-man crew, it had a top speed of 80 km/h and a range of 320 km. Dimensions were: length, 4.8 m; width, 1.95 m; and height, 1.75 m.

SdKfz 222 late model. The later model of the 222 was much used by the Deutsche Afrika Korps (DAK). It had thicker armour, up to 30 mm on the nose and 10 mm on the front of the turret.

SdKfz 260 and SdKfz 261 kleiner panzerfunkwagen, 1940 (*Below right*). A development of the SdKfz 222 was this small radio car for use by unit headquarters in communicating with higher formations. The 260 had a medium range radio set and used a rod aerial, while the 261 had a longer range set which required a frame aerial (as seen here). However, later models of the 261 also had a rod aerial. The 260 weighed 3.82 tons, and the 261 3.86 tons. The crew was normally four men (driver, commander and two radio operators). The extra man and radio meant that no armament could be carried apart from the crews' personal weapons.

Schildkröte amphibious recce vehicle, 1941 (*Left and far left*). During the years 1941–44, Hans Trippel of Trippelwerke carried out development work on a series of amphibious recce vehicles (see drawing). Three prototypes were produced, all known as Schildkröte (Turtle), including a turretless munitions carrier (seen in the photograph). Although they were tested by the Wehrmacht in the autumn of 1944, they were not put into production.

SdKfz 231 schwerer panzerspähwagen, 6rad, 1935. Developed from the PzSpWg G3aP of 1932 (see Part 3, Section 7, page 85), this heavy armoured car saw active service at the start of the war in the campaigns in Poland and France. It had been issued before the war to the developing recce forces and used extensively during the annexation of Austria and Czechoslovakia. The four-man, $5\frac{1}{2}$-ton 6 × 4 car had a top speed of 70 km/h and a range of 250 km. Dimensions were: length, 5.61 m; width, 1.85 m; and height, 2.24 m. The armour thickness was some 8 mm. The armament was one 2 cm KwK30 plus a 7.92 mm MG13.

SdKfz 232 schwerer panzerspähwagen (funkwagen) 6rad, 1936 (*Below and below left*). Two good photographs showing the radio version of the 231 6rad which was fitted with a long-range 100 watt radio and its distinctive frame aerial. Note how the frame has a central bearing which enables the turret to rotate fully underneath the aerial array.

SdKfz 263 panzerfunkwagen 6rad. The main differences between this model and the 231/232 was that the turret was fixed and mounted just a single MG13, the rest of the space being taken up with radio equipment, plus an extra radio operator (the crew was five – two drivers and three turret crew). It weighed about $\frac{1}{4}$ ton less than the 232.

SdKfz 231 schwerer panzerspähwagen 8rad, 1937 (*Below and below left*). Most powerful of all German armoured cars used in World War 2 were those on an 8 × 8 chassis, the first of which was developed in 1935–36 and put into production in 1937. The 8.3-ton (7.55 tons unladen), four-man armoured car had one 2 cm KwK30 and one MG34 mounted coaxially and fired by pedals on the gunner's footrest. The car had a top speed of 85 km/h and a range of 270 km. The photograph *below* shows a later production model; note the spaced armour fitted on to the nose.

SdKfz 232 schwerer panzerspähwagen 8rad (funkwagen) (*Above and left*). This model was almost identical to the 231 as far as armament and traversing turret are concerned. The radio car was fitted with medium range radio equipment together with the usual large frame aerial, again with the central bearing to allow the turret unimpeded traverse.

SdKfz 232 late model. This photograph shows a late version of the funkwagen in which the frame aerial array had been replaced by a rod aerial on the turret roof and a 'star' type aerial on the centre of the rear deck (not easy to see in the photograph – there were six small projecting rods at the top of the main antenna rod, resembling a star).

SdKfz 233 schwerer panzerspähwagen 8rad, 1942. Entering service in late 1942, this version of the 8 × 8 heavy armoured car had a short 7.5 cm KwK 37 L/24 gun mounted in place of the usual turret. The 7.5 cm gun had only limited traverse. This model greatly increased the offensive fire support capability of recce squadrons, normally being issued on a scale of six per squadron. The fully laden weight was 8.58 tons, and it had a top speed of 85 km/h and a range of 300 km. The crew was three men. Dimensions were: length, 5.85 m; width, 2.2 m; height, 2.25 m.

SdKfz 263 panzerfunkwagen 8rad, 1938. As with the six-wheel version (the SdKfz 263, page 153), this heavy, long range command car had a fixed turret and no main armament other than an MG34. This allowed far more space inside for its crew of five, plus its long range radio. The 263 was issued to signals units of panzer and motorised divisions and to some higher formations.

Ballistik-Messfahrzeug. Also based on the eight-wheel SdKfz 231 chassis, this fully armoured observation vehicle was presumably designed for work on the observation of the effects of artillery fire at close range. It was found at an artillery proving ground at the end of the war.

SdKfz 234/1 schwerer panzerspähwagen 8rad, 1944. Work on a successor to the 231 series began in the early 1940s, and the first models entered production in 1943. The new series were very similar to the previous one but were of monocoque construction (ie: an integral body and chassis, sharing all stresses and strains) of thicker armour (up to 30 mm on the front of the hull and turret), and had better performance. The engine chosen was the Tatra 220 bhp diesel which gave the $11\frac{1}{2}$-ton vehicle a top speed of 80 km/h. Initially its range was 600 km, but this was increased to 1,000 km by fitting a larger fuel tank. The SdKfz 234/1, seen here, mounted a 2 cm KwK38 gun with a coaxial MG42. It had the usual wire mesh screen over the open-topped turret. With a length of 6 m and height of 2.1 m, it was somewhat lower and longer than the previous series. It was 2.4 m wide. Note how the separate mudguards have now been joined up.

SdKfz 234/2 schwerer panzerspähwagen 8rad, 1943, Puma. One of the few German armoured cars to be given a name, the Puma was designed to give the recce forces a vehicle capable of standing up to the Russian light and medium tanks. It mounted a 5 cm KwK 39/1 gun and a coaxial MG42 in a turret originally designed for the Leopard light tank. Only 101 Pumas were produced, a very small percentage of the 2,000 plus SdKfz series production. The four-man armoured car had an all up weight of 11.74 tons. Dimensions were: length, 6.8 m; width, 2.4 m; and height, 2.28 m. It saw service in four panzer divisions on both the Russian and European fronts, being organised into panzerspähwagen companies each of 25 Pumas.

SdKfz 234/3 schwerer panzerspähwagen 8rad, 1944. Taking over the role from the SdKfz 233, heavy support for the recce was provided by this open-topped turretless version of the SdKfz 234 series which mounted a 7.5 cm KwK 51 short-barrelled gun with only limited traverse. The 10-ton car had a crew of four, and was 6 m long, 2.33 m wide, and 2.36 m high.

SdKfz 247 schwerer panzerkraftwagen, 1941. To give its full title, this wheeled APC was known as the Schwerer Geländegängiger Gepanzerter Personenkraftwagen (s.gl.gpPkw) SdKfz 247. It was based on the heavy passenger car chassis and there were both 6 × 4 (Ausf A) and 4 × 4 (Ausf B) versions; the photograph shows the former. It could take six men, and was used by the battalion commanders of recce battalions as an armoured staff car.

SdKfz 234/4 schwerer panzerspähwagen 8rad, 1944. Personally ordered by Hitler to boost up the Puma and SdKfz 234/3, this model mounted the longer, more powerful 7.5 cm Pak 40 gun, complete with shield. Only a limited number actually saw any operational service.

Strassenpanzerwagen, 1940. The SS made up a number of improvised armoured cars using various commercial lorries. One model incorporated the turret of a French tank, but others, like the one in this photograph, were open-topped with a machine gun in the right front plate.

Kfz 4 leichter truppenluftschützkraftwagen, 1937 (*Below and below left*). One of the smallest AA Flak vehicles designed for the protection of motorised convoys was this light troop air defence vehicle which used the standard light personnel carrier built by Stoewer of Stettin which appeared in five variants between 1937 and 1940, of which the Kfz 4 was but one. It mounted two MG42 on a dual mount (Zwillingslafette 36 – see photograph *below left*) with an aircraft sight and had all-round traverse.

FlaK 38(Sf) auf schwerer geländegängiger einheits PKW. A number of heavy 4 × 4 Horch cross-country personnel carriers were converted to FlaK vehicles, by mounting a single 2 cm FlaK 38 (or FlaK 30) within the standard body.

FlaK 38, other versions. Two other FlaK 38 conversions to the AA role are shown here, a Krupps Protze 6 × 4 truck (*right*), and on a Mercedes Benz L4500A (*far right*).

Schwerer Minenraumfahrzeug, 1944 (*Centre right*). An enormous 130-ton vehicle, built by Krupps, it had wheels 2.7 m in diameter! It was only ever produced in prototype.

Captured enemy vehicles. The Germans, like everyone else, made use of captured equipment when it was taken in a serviceable condition. These photographs show a British Humber Mark II, captured in the Western Desert, with a Nazi flag suitably placed for air to ground recognition (*bottom left*), and a French AMD Panhard 178 in action in Russia (*below right*), and an AEC armoured command vehicle (ACV) in service with the DAK (*below*). Nicknamed *Max* and *Moritz* after characters in a childrens' story, two Mammoths, as the Germans called the British AEC armoured command vehicles (ACV), were taken at the same time as the DAK captured Generals O'Connor and Neame in April 1941. In fact, no less a person than the Desert Fox himself used one ACV as his command vehicle.

Italy

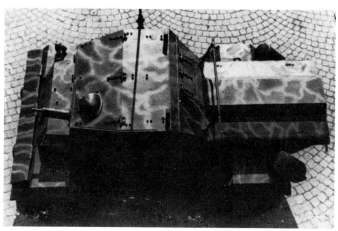

Lince scout car, 1944 (*Top and centre right*). Almost an exact copy of the British Daimler Dingo scout car, the Lince was built by Lancia after the armistice with Italy, and was used by units of the RSI (Republica Sociale Italiana, the Fascist administration in northern Italy set up in September 1943 by Mussolini after the armistice). It was armed with a single Breda 8 mm machine gun and had a crew of two. Its weight was 3.14 tons and it was 3.25 m long, 1.75 m wide, and 1.65 m high. About 250 were built.

Autoblinda AB 40, 1940. The first prototype was tested in mid-1939, it was designed to replace the ageing Lancia IZ (see Part 3, Section 9). It had four-wheel drive and all four wheels were independently sprung. It could be driven in either direction, having dual driving controls, one set at each end. The 6.85-ton vehicle had a crew of four and mounted three Breda 8 mm machine guns, two on the turret and a third in the hull rear, firing over the back decks. Dimensions were: length, 5.2 m; width, 1.93 m; and height, 2.44 m. Note also the spare wheels which were mounted on free bearings on the sides in such a position as to help in crossing obstacles, as the photograph shows.

AB 40, rear driving position. This photograph shows the rear driving position with the ball-mounted 8 mm gun alongside the driving controls.

Autoblinda AB 41, 1941 (*Left and below*). The major difference in the AB 41 to the AB 40 was the mounting of a 20 mm gun with a coaxially-mounted machine gun, in place of the dual machine guns. It was the most widely used Italian armoured car of the war, seeing service in North Africa, Russia, Italy and Hungary. It weighed 7.4 tons and had a top speed of 78 km/h.

SPA 42, 1942. This wheeled SP gun (prototype) was derived from the AB 41. It had an open top in which a 47 mm gun was mounted, complete with shield.

Autoblinda AB 43, 1943. Final version of the SPA-Ansaldo armoured car was the AB 43, which now had a 47 mm gun as its main armament. It weighed 7.47 tons, and had a top speed of 90 km/h and a range of 535 km. It was built only in limited numbers, production being halted by the Italian surrender. Note the buggy whip aerial at the rear.

Carro Protetto AS 37. Based on the AS 37 light desert truck, this armoured personnel carrier could carry ten men and a driver. It had an 8 mm machine gun at the rear and a front-mounted engine.

Trialce Moto Gucci, 1941. This was a motor tricycle powered by the front end of a Moto Gucci motorbike. It mounted a single machine gun – note the machine gun ground mounting tripod strapped on the rear.

Autoblinda Vespa Caproni, 1941. This odd-looking little AFV had four wheels in a diamond layout and mounted a single machine gun in the centre of its small cab. Dimensions were: length, 12 ft 10 ins; width, 6 ft 6 ins; and height, 6 ft 1 in.

Lancia autocannone da 90 (90/53). Dropsided Lancia 3RO unarmoured lorry, mounting a Cannone da 90/53 M41 anti-aircraft gun, with large pedestal mount jacks shown in the ready-for-action position.

Lancia 3RO/105, 1940. This time, the Lancia 3RO lorry chassis has a 105 mm howitzer in the rear, firing over the tailboard.

Panzerserra Bunker

Panzerserra´s blog about military models in 1/35 scale. World War I and World War II

About me | Links | Tips & Tricks | von Serra - the new mascot !!!

Camionetta AS 42 Sahariana with Breda 20mm gun - a case report

Gents...

I'm still in the process of moving home and my bench is disassembled. I'm suffering a serious crisis of styrene and resin abstinence.

To keep my bunker active and interesting, I will introduce to you guys a building of 2007 that I really liked: An Italian girl: **Camionetta AS-42 Sahariana**, from Italeri, in 1/35 scale.

DISCL

The pub
informa
fascism
regimes
the re
accura
these reg

A public
ou inf
nazismo
outros re
entendida
históric
estes reg

Total view:

Panzerserra Bunker

Panzerserra´s blog about military models in 1/35 scale. World War I and World War II

Camionetta AS 42 Sahariana with Breda 20mm gun - a case report

Gents...

I'm still in the process of moving home and my bench is disassembled. I'm suffering a serious crisis of styrene and resin abstinence.

To keep my bunker active and interesting, I will introduce to you guys a building of 2007 that I really liked: An Italian girl: **Camionetta AS-42 Sahariana**, from Italeri, in 1/35 scale.

Camionetta SPA 43, 1942. Ideal for fast operations in the desert, this long, low, 4-ton vehicle had a boat-shaped hull and mounted either one or two 20 mm AA guns, which could be used in both the air and ground roles. Note the rows of jerricans (400 litres, which doubled the range to 800 km), on the sides and sand troughs carried each side of the rear-mounted engine. Used by mechanised cavalry units for long-distance patrol work. It was also called the Sahariana Ante Aera SPA. Dimensions were: length, 18 ft 10 ins; width, 7 ft; and height, 6 ft.

Sahariana Corta 75/27 (*Below*). Another desert vehicle was this short wheelbase gun tractor mounting a 75 mm gun on a pedestal with its shield, but with no armour.

SPA 35 AA lorry (*Above*). Another example of a gun mounted on a lorry chassis without any armour is this 20 mm AA gun on an SPA cargo truck.

Machine gun mount. Good view of a twin heavy machine gun mount specially designed for mounting on the rear of a lorry.

Autocannone Blindada Tipo 102. This was a short, low, six-wheeled armoured vehicle on which a 102 mm naval gun with its shield was mounted so as to fire over the top of the cut down box-like hull. The side panels folded down to allow the gun to traverse.

Breda AA 90/53, 1942. This model was built in 1942 and had an Ansaldo 90/53 gun mounted on a six-wheel Breda chassis, which had large jacks at the rear for stable firing. This particular gun was abandoned by the Italians in Sicily, near San Michele, in August 1943.

Japan

Ford conversion, 1941. Converted from a 1½-ton Ford truck by the Japanese, this vehicle was 19 ft 9 ins long, 7 ft 10 ins wide, and 9 ft high. Note the hatch on the front of the bevelled top; there was a similar one at the rear.

Ford conversion, 1941. Another Ford truck conversion, this time with a round hatch at the front and a small, many-sided turret at the rear.

Poland

Warsaw uprising armoured car, 1944.
One of the improvised armoured vehicles used by the Poles in their valiant uprising in Warsaw on 1 August 1944 when 42,500 of General Bor-Komorowski's Home Army, plus civilians and the Communist People's Army, won two thirds of the city in 20 hours of hard fighting. Although the AFV is described as a 'tank', there appear to be wheels, at least at the front. Note also what looks like the Stars and Stripes on the top and the Polish Eagle on the front.

Warsaw uprising improvised armoured car, 1944. This improvised armoured car was captured from the Germans by the Home Army and used by them, but it is not clear who put on the armour. After fierce fighting, the Poles had to surrender as the Russians did not produce the support for which General Komorowski had been hoping.

Captured armoured car, 1944. With the Polish Eagle now emblazoned on its front plate, this German armoured car was captured during the battle for Warsaw. In all, the Poles suffered 15,000 killed, whilst the Germans lost 10,000 killed and 16,000 missing or wounded.

Russia

Russo-German co-operation. These three photographs were taken on 2 October 1939 at Brest Litowsk in Poland, while the Germans and Russians, still 'Allies', were holding a conference to decide upon how Poland should be divided. In all cases, the armoured cars are BA 20 (V), the Commander's model of the BA 20.

BA 64 scout car, 1942 (*Right*). The only new armoured car to be standardised by the Russians during World War 2 was this small 2.36 ton scout car. It was a two-man car, designed mainly for liaison, but was also used for recce. Produced by GAZ, it shows distinct German influence in its armour arrangement. It had a top speed of 50 mph and a range of 280 miles. Dimensions were: length, 12 ft; width, 5 ft; and height, 6 ft 3 ins.

BA 64 with heavy machine gun (*Top right*). A heavy 12.7 mm DShK 1938 machine gun has been mounted on this BA 64 atop the small, open-topped turret. This most useful machine gun was used for a variety of purposes, one being as secondary armament on various Russian tanks.

BA 64 D, 1942 (*Above*). Turretless version of the BA 46 which was used by airborne troops, this particular car has clearly been taken over by the Yanks.

BA 10s under scrutiny (*Left*). Russian armoured car crews show off their six-wheeled BA 10s to admiring British troops. It is thought that this photograph was taken in Persia in 1941, after Russian and British forces had entered Teheran in the middle of September.

A Russian workshop repairs AFVs.
Good photograph of work in progress on
BA 10s in a Russian workshop during
World War 2.

BA 10M under new management. Now
sporting German crosses, this late model
BA 10M has just set fire to a Russian
farmhouse.

Improvised armoured car, at Leningrad. A detachment of Red Army soldiers, accompanied by an improvised armoured car, move to take up their positions during the defence of Leningrad. The main armament of the car appears to be a heavy machine gun on an AA mount.

Quad machine gun mounting. Finnish troops inspect a captured Russian AA lorry after destroying the Soviet 44th Division on the Suomassalmi front, January 1940. The quadruple mounting of the M1910 7.62 mm machine gun was used both on lorries and sledges during the Russo-Finnish War.

Lorry mounted AA gun. A Russian crew get ready to engage enemy aircraft with their 76.2 mm Model 1931 anti-aircraft gun, which was one of the oldest types in use in the Red Army during World War 2.

Katyusha rocket launcher. A crew reload an M13 launcher mounted on a ZIS-6 truck. The M13 could carry 16 × 132 mm rockets in pairs, eight under and eight on top of the I-section steel rails, the lower rockets being held on by studs.

Lend-Lease scout cars (*Below*). The Russians used American White scout cars during World War 2, as seen here during the main Russian offensive.

BA 10s in Turkish service (*Bottom*). These BA 10s were photographed during a military parade in Turkey in April 1940.

USA

Chrysler scout car, 1941. This very simple 'add-on armour' scout car was built by Chrysler for convoy protection or for use as a small APC. The armoured body was bolted on to a $1\frac{1}{2}$-ton 4×4 Dodge truck chassis. It did not go into production because the narrow body and high silhouette were significant drawbacks.

Observation Post Tender, T1 (*Below right*). Ford built this small (12 ft long) vehicle intended for use by intelligence gathering personnel.

Observation Post Tender T2 (*Below*). The photograph was taken during testing at the Aberdeen Proving Grounds in late 1941. The only differences to the T1 appear to be the folding armoured gunshields in place of the windscreen and slightly more armour. It was not put into production. The T2 weighed 6,600 lbs fully loaded and was powered by a 90 hp Ford engine.

Smart scout car, 1941. First in a line of armoured Jeeps, the Smart Engineering Company of Detroit designed and built this armoured version on a standard Willys chassis.

T 25 scout car. The second version produced by Smart Engineering, had a lower windscreen and some side protection. It was designated T 25.

T25E2, 1941. This was the fifth stage in the development of the armoured jeep/scout car. There is now considerably more armour (985 lbs making up nearly a third of the vehicle's weight), but the driver and crew still appear to look over the top of the armour rather than through their vision slits.

T25E3 early model. The Jeep has now become almost completely armoured. There is full armour all-round at over-head height, with observation/firing ports and access doors.

T25E3 second model. Last version of the T25 series was very like the earlier model except that there was better cooling for the radiator. The side and rear armour is hinged and is hanging down on this photograph.

Home-made armored Jeeps. 82nd Airborne designed and built the first of these 'home made' armored cars (*below*), which carries a .50 Browning and was used for recce work. The second (*left*) was photographed in Northern France in 1944 and mounts a .30 Browning.

Staghound mock-up T17E1, 1942 (*Above*). Chevrolet built this armoured car to British specifications for such roles as convoy protection and recce. It was not used by the US Army, but the British bought over 2,800 of them. As this mock-up shows, it had a very symmetrical shape.

T24 scout car, 1942 (*Left*). During the development of the Jeep, a ¾-ton six-wheeled version was built for use as a cargo carrier, ambulance, etc. Smart Engineering produced an armoured version, weighing 5,450 lbs fully loaded – some 2,350 lbs heavier than the unarmoured cargo version. It was 14 ft long, and was armed with a .50 Browning on a pedestal mount. After testing at the Aberdeen Proving Grounds, it was decided that there was no requirement for the T24 and it did not go into production.

All-round views of the Staghound.
Designed as a five-man armored car, the
13.7-ton Staghound was a robust and
extremely useful AFV. The main
armament was a 37 mm gun with a
coaxially-mounted .30 calibre machine gun
and .30 in the hull and on an AA mount.
The maximum armour's thickness was
45 mm. The Staghound had a top speed of
56 mph and a road range of 450 miles. It
was 18 ft long, 8 ft 10 ins wide, and 7 ft 9 ins
high.

Staghound in Ghent, 1944. The British used Staghounds in all theatres. This photograph shows the GOC of 7th Armoured Division, General Verney, arriving at Ghent Town Hall on 8 September 1944 after his famous Division (The Desert Rats) had liberated the Belgian city.

Pilot model of T17E2. The new turret, designed by Frazer-Nash in England, on a Staghound chassis, mounted twin .50 calibre Brownings in an AA mode.

T17E2, 1942. Good view of the Frazer-Nash D8394 open-turret with the twin .50 calibre machine guns installed. The gun mount would allow the guns to elevate to 75 degrees and depress to 10 degrees while the hydraulically operated turret had 360 degrees traverse. One hundred were produced and some are still in service around the world.

T17E3. The T17E1 was modified to take a 75 mm howitzer, but it was only produced in prototype form and did not enter production.

Staghound Bantu. This version of the Staghound had electrical mine locator rollers mounted fore and aft.

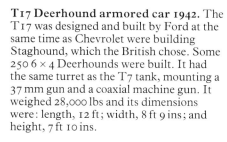

T17 Deerhound armored car 1942. The T17 was designed and built by Ford at the same time as Chevrolet were building Staghound, which the British chose. Some 250 6 × 4 Deerhounds were built. It had the same turret as the T7 tank, mounting a 37 mm gun and a coaxial machine gun. It weighed 28,000 lbs and its dimensions were: length, 12 ft; width, 8 ft 9 ins; and height, 7 ft 10 ins.

T19 armored car, 1942. Rear view of the Chevrolet-built 28,000-lb armored car, which, like the T17, had the turret of the T7 light tank. Its 104 hp engine gave it a top speed of 50 mph and it had armour up to $\frac{1}{2}$ in thick.

T19E1 armored car, 1942. Developed from the T19, the T19E1 had an improved mounting for the 37 mm gun. It weighed 1,000 lbs more than the T19. Dimensions were: length, 18 ft; width, 10 ft; and height, 8 ft.

T21 armored car, 1942. Most American firms seem to have built 6 × 4 armoured cars in 1942! This one was built by Studebaker and was also known as the T43 Gun Motor Carriage. It was not as successful on test as the Ford-built T22.

T22 armored car, 1942. This Ford-built 6 × 4 mounted an M6 37 mm gun in an M23A1 mount with a coaxial .30 calibre Browning. This four-man car had a collapsible driver's cupola (seen here raised). It was: 15 ft long, 8 ft 4 ins wide, and 6 ft 8 ins high. It was much lighter at only 15,000 lbs than the 6 × 6 armoured cars produced by other American firms.

All-round views of the M8 Greyhound armored car, 1943. The T22 led on to the T22E1 and then the T22E2 armored car which was standardised as the M8 Greyhound. It was America's most used armoured car of World War 2, 8,523 being built by the Ford Motor Company. Very fast (56 mph) and very quiet, it was an ideal recce vehicle, and was used extensively by the US Army. It was powered by a Hercules JXD petrol engine, mounted in the rear. Dimensions were: length, 16 ft 5 ins; width, 8 ft 4 ins; and height, 7 ft 5 ins. *Below* is a close-up of driver's and co-driver's cabs on the Greyhound.

The M8 in action. In all three photographs of the Greyhound in action, a 'skate' ring mount has been added on to the turret to take a .50 calibre heavy Browning machine gun. Clearly, there was little room for stowage inside the turret of the M8 and everything has to be suspended around it. The photographs chart the US Army's progress through France and on into Germany, through scenes of continuing devastation.

M20 armored utility car, 1943. Nearly 4,000 M20 utility cars were built by Ford. Also called the T26 and, for a time, the Armored Utility Car M10, this versatile vehicle mounted a .50 calibre heavy Browning machine gun on a skate ring mount in place of the M8 turret. The M20 was 15 ft 8 ins long, 8 ft 5 ins wide, and 6 ft 6 ins high.

M20 with experimental machine gun mount (*Below*). This version of the M20 mounted twin .50 Brownings.

Carriage GMC T69 (*Above*). This version of the M8 had quad Maxson .50 calibre machine guns in a power-operated turret for use as an AA weapon. The photograph shows the rear of the turret with the guns lowered.

T23 armored car, 1942. Chrysler Corporation also built an armoured car in competition with Ford's T22, which was basically of similar design. Note the high cowl over the complete width of the armoured car for the driver and co-driver, which, unfortunately, interfered with the depression of the main armament.

T28 armored car, 1944. Sometimes called the Wolfhound, this good looking armoured car was built as a successor to the T19E1 by Chevrolet. It weighed only 14,500 lbs and had a top speed in excess of 60 mph. It was later redesigned as the M38 armored car. The main armament was still a 37 mm gun.

M38 modified, 1946. An interesting post-war modification of the Wolfhound involved fitting the turret from the M24 Chaffee light tank, which mounted a 76 mm gun.

T66 75 mm Gun Motor Carriage. Yet another variation, this time with a 75 mm gun in an open topped turret on the T19E1 chassis.

T13 armored car, 1942. Based on the experience gained designing the Trackless Tank (see Part 3, Section 17, US inter-war armored cars), Reo built two prototypes in 1941, mounting a 37 mm gun and a machine gun in the turret, plus one machine gun in the hull. T13 weighed about 32,000 lbs and was reputed to have a top speed of 60 mph. It was not put into production.

T18 armored car, 1942. Large and heavy (over 26 tons), the T18, built by the Yellow Coach Division of General Motors, led directly on to the T18E2, which became known as the Boarhound. The T18E1 was not built.

T18E2 Boarhound armoured car, 1942. The T18E2 followed on from the T18 pilot model as the T18E1 was not built. It was exceptionally large and heavy, weighing over 26.8 tons and measuring over 20 ft in length and 10 ft wide. High off the ground, it could ford through 4 ft of water with ease. Its main armament was a 57 mm (6-pdr) gun, with a coaxial machine gun and another in the front plate. Its armour thickness was up to 2 ins in parts. It was built for the British, but only 30 were completed.

T55 3-inch Gun Motor Carriage, 1942. Also called 'Cook's Cozy Cabin'! This very large vehicle – it was over $25\frac{1}{2}$ ft long – had a 3-inch gun mounted in an open-topped hull on a T18 chassis.

T27 armored car, 1943. Studebaker built this racy looking armoured car, which weighed only $7\frac{1}{2}$ tons fully stowed. It could cruise along at over 60 mph and had armour up to $\frac{3}{4}$ in thick. The T27 steered on both front axles.

Baker Tank, 1942. This project was started but never completed. The large coil springs on the wheels were intended to enable the vehicle to 'jump' across gaps. There was also a 4×4 version.

Top row, left to right: **German armour in Austria.** Adolf Hitler reviews his armoured might in the Ringstrasse Vienna, as a pair of SdKfz 221 light armoured cars motor past the saluting base. **America's steel horses on the march.** M1 armored cars belonging to the first United States cavalry regiment to be mechanised seen on manoeuvres. **Red Square parade.** BA32 armoured cars on parade in Red Square during one of the last parades to be held there before the Great Patriotic War. *Middle*: **'The last time I saw Paris'.** American M8 Greyhound armored cars parade through the Arc de Triomphe and down the Champs-Elysées after the liberation of the French capital, 25 August 1945. *Bottom*: **Victory parade, London.** A column of Dingos move under the shadow of the Tower of London on their way to the Mall, where the salute was taken by Their Majesties. The formation signs on the front plates denote their VIP occupants.

Index